I0351440

C-1077 CAREER EXAMINATION SERIES

This is your
PASSBOOK for...

Administrator

Test Preparation Study Guide
Questions & Answers

NLC®
NATIONAL LEARNING CORPORATION®

National Learning Corporation

212 Michael Drive, Syosset, NY 11791
(516) 921-8888 • www.passbooks.com
E-mail: info@passbooks.com

PASSBOOK® SERIES

THE *PASSBOOK® SERIES* has been created to prepare applicants and candidates for the ultimate academic battlefield – the examination room.

At some time in our lives, each and every one of us may be required to take an examination – for validation, matriculation, admission, qualification, registration, certification, or licensure.

Based on the assumption that every applicant or candidate has met the basic formal educational standards, has taken the required number of courses, and read the necessary texts, the *PASSBOOK® SERIES* furnishes the one special preparation which may assure passing with confidence, instead of failing with insecurity. Examination questions – together with answers – are furnished as the basic vehicle for study so that the mysteries of the examination and its compounding difficulties may be eliminated or diminished by a sure method.

This book is meant to help you pass your examination provided that you qualify and are serious in your objective.

The entire field is reviewed through the huge store of content information which is succinctly presented through a provocative and challenging approach – the question-and-answer method.

A climate of success is established by furnishing the correct answers at the end of each test.

You soon learn to recognize types of questions, forms of questions, and patterns of questioning. You may even begin to anticipate expected outcomes.

You perceive that many questions are repeated or adapted so that you can gain acute insights, which may enable you to score many sure points.

You learn how to confront new questions, or types of questions, and to attack them confidently and work out the correct answers.

You note objectives and emphases, and recognize pitfalls and dangers, so that you may make positive educational adjustments.

Moreover, you are kept fully informed in relation to new concepts, methods, practices, and directions in the field.

You discover that you are actually taking the examination all the time: you are preparing for the examination by "taking" an examination, not by reading extraneous and/or supererogatory textbooks.

In short, this PASSBOOK®, used directedly, should be an important factor in helping you to pass your test.

ADMINISTRATOR

DUTIES
Responsible for the maintenance of basic administrative duties related to services provided in local and state agencies.

SCOPE OF THE EXAMINATION
The written test is designed to test for knowledge, skills and/or abilities in such areas as:

1. Administration;
2. Preparing written material;
3. Program planning and evaluation; and
4. Understanding and interpreting written material.

HOW TO TAKE A TEST

I. YOU MUST PASS AN EXAMINATION

A. WHAT EVERY CANDIDATE SHOULD KNOW

Examination applicants often ask us for help in preparing for the written test. What can I study in advance? What kinds of questions will be asked? How will the test be given? How will the papers be graded?

As an applicant for a civil service examination, you may be wondering about some of these things. Our purpose here is to suggest effective methods of advance study and to describe civil service examinations.

Your chances for success on this examination can be increased if you know how to prepare. Those "pre-examination jitters" can be reduced if you know what to expect. You can even experience an adventure in good citizenship if you know why civil service exams are given.

B. WHY ARE CIVIL SERVICE EXAMINATIONS GIVEN?

Civil service examinations are important to you in two ways. As a citizen, you want public jobs filled by employees who know how to do their work. As a job seeker, you want a fair chance to compete for that job on an equal footing with other candidates. The best-known means of accomplishing this two-fold goal is the competitive examination.

Exams are widely publicized throughout the nation. They may be administered for jobs in federal, state, city, municipal, town or village governments or agencies.

Any citizen may apply, with some limitations, such as the age or residence of applicants. Your experience and education may be reviewed to see whether you meet the requirements for the particular examination. When these requirements exist, they are reasonable and applied consistently to all applicants. Thus, a competitive examination may cause you some uneasiness now, but it is your privilege and safeguard.

C. HOW ARE CIVIL SERVICE EXAMS DEVELOPED?

Examinations are carefully written by trained technicians who are specialists in the field known as "psychological measurement," in consultation with recognized authorities in the field of work that the test will cover. These experts recommend the subject matter areas or skills to be tested; only those knowledges or skills important to your success on the job are included. The most reliable books and source materials available are used as references. Together, the experts and technicians judge the difficulty level of the questions.

Test technicians know how to phrase questions so that the problem is clearly stated. Their ethics do not permit "trick" or "catch" questions. Questions may have been tried out on sample groups, or subjected to statistical analysis, to determine their usefulness.

Written tests are often used in combination with performance tests, ratings of training and experience, and oral interviews. All of these measures combine to form the best-known means of finding the right person for the right job.

II. HOW TO PASS THE WRITTEN TEST

A. NATURE OF THE EXAMINATION

To prepare intelligently for civil service examinations, you should know how they differ from school examinations you have taken. In school you were assigned certain definite pages to read or subjects to cover. The examination questions were quite detailed and usually emphasized memory. Civil service exams, on the other hand, try to discover your present ability to perform the duties of a position, plus your potentiality to learn these duties. In other words, a civil service exam attempts to predict how successful you will be. Questions cover such a broad area that they cannot be as minute and detailed as school exam questions.

In the public service similar kinds of work, or positions, are grouped together in one "class." This process is known as *position-classification.* All the positions in a class are paid according to the salary range for that class. One class title covers all of these positions, and they are all tested by the same examination.

B. FOUR BASIC STEPS

1) Study the announcement

How, then, can you know what subjects to study? Our best answer is: "Learn as much as possible about the class of positions for which you've applied." The exam will test the knowledge, skills and abilities needed to do the work.

Your most valuable source of information about the position you want is the official exam announcement. This announcement lists the training and experience qualifications. Check these standards and apply only if you come reasonably close to meeting them.

The brief description of the position in the examination announcement offers some clues to the subjects which will be tested. Think about the job itself. Review the duties in your mind. Can you perform them, or are there some in which you are rusty? Fill in the blank spots in your preparation.

Many jurisdictions preview the written test in the exam announcement by including a section called "Knowledge and Abilities Required," "Scope of the Examination," or some similar heading. Here you will find out specifically what fields will be tested.

2) Review your own background

Once you learn in general what the position is all about, and what you need to know to do the work, ask yourself which subjects you already know fairly well and which need improvement. You may wonder whether to concentrate on improving your strong areas or on building some background in your fields of weakness. When the announcement has specified "some knowledge" or "considerable knowledge," or has used adjectives like "beginning principles of..." or "advanced ... methods," you can get a clue as to the number and difficulty of questions to be asked in any given field. More questions, and hence broader coverage, would be included for those subjects which are more important in the work. Now weigh your strengths and weaknesses against the job requirements and prepare accordingly.

3) Determine the level of the position

Another way to tell how intensively you should prepare is to understand the level of the job for which you are applying. Is it the entering level? In other words, is this the position in which beginners in a field of work are hired? Or is it an intermediate or advanced level? Sometimes this is indicated by such words as "Junior" or "Senior" in the class title. Other jurisdictions use Roman numerals to designate the level – Clerk I, Clerk II, for example. The word "Supervisor" sometimes appears in the title. If the level is not indicated by the title, check the description of duties. Will you be working under very close supervision, or will you have responsibility for independent decisions in this work?

4) Choose appropriate study materials

Now that you know the subjects to be examined and the relative amount of each subject to be covered, you can choose suitable study materials. For beginning level jobs, or even advanced ones, if you have a pronounced weakness in some aspect of your training, read a modern, standard textbook in that field. Be sure it is up to date and has general coverage. Such books are normally available at your library, and the librarian will be glad to help you locate one. For entry-level positions, questions of appropriate difficulty are chosen – neither highly advanced questions, nor those too simple. Such questions require careful thought but not advanced training.

If the position for which you are applying is technical or advanced, you will read more advanced, specialized material. If you are already familiar with the basic principles of your field, elementary textbooks would waste your time. Concentrate on advanced textbooks and technical periodicals. Think through the concepts and review difficult problems in your field.

These are all general sources. You can get more ideas on your own initiative, following these leads. For example, training manuals and publications of the government agency which employs workers in your field can be useful, particularly for technical and professional positions. A letter or visit to the government department involved may result in more specific study suggestions, and certainly will provide you with a more definite idea of the exact nature of the position you are seeking.

III. KINDS OF TESTS

Tests are used for purposes other than measuring knowledge and ability to perform specified duties. For some positions, it is equally important to test ability to make adjustments to new situations or to profit from training. In others, basic mental abilities not dependent on information are essential. Questions which test these things may not appear as pertinent to the duties of the position as those which test for knowledge and information. Yet they are often highly important parts of a fair examination. For very general questions, it is almost impossible to help you direct your study efforts. What we can do is to point out some of the more common of these general abilities needed in public service positions and describe some typical questions.

1) General information

Broad, general information has been found useful for predicting job success in some kinds of work. This is tested in a variety of ways, from vocabulary lists to questions about current events. Basic background in some field of work, such as sociology or economics, may be sampled in a group of questions. Often these are principles which have become familiar to most persons through exposure rather than through formal training. It is difficult to advise you how to study for these questions; being alert to the world around you is our best suggestion.

2) Verbal ability

An example of an ability needed in many positions is verbal or language ability. Verbal ability is, in brief, the ability to use and understand words. Vocabulary and grammar tests are typical measures of this ability. Reading comprehension or paragraph interpretation questions are common in many kinds of civil service tests. You are given a paragraph of written material and asked to find its central meaning.

3) Numerical ability

Number skills can be tested by the familiar arithmetic problem, by checking paired lists of numbers to see which are alike and which are different, or by interpreting charts and graphs. In the latter test, a graph may be printed in the test booklet which you are asked to use as the basis for answering questions.

4) Observation

A popular test for law-enforcement positions is the observation test. A picture is shown to you for several minutes, then taken away. Questions about the picture test your ability to observe both details and larger elements.

5) Following directions

In many positions in the public service, the employee must be able to carry out written instructions dependably and accurately. You may be given a chart with several columns, each column listing a variety of information. The questions require you to carry out directions involving the information given in the chart.

6) Skills and aptitudes

Performance tests effectively measure some manual skills and aptitudes. When the skill is one in which you are trained, such as typing or shorthand, you can practice. These tests are often very much like those given in business school or high school courses. For many of the other skills and aptitudes, however, no short-time preparation can be made. Skills and abilities natural to you or that you have developed throughout your lifetime are being tested.

Many of the general questions just described provide all the data needed to answer the questions and ask you to use your reasoning ability to find the answers. Your best preparation for these tests, as well as for tests of facts and ideas, is to be at your physical and mental best. You, no doubt, have your own methods of getting into an exam-taking mood and keeping "in shape." The next section lists some ideas on this subject.

IV. KINDS OF QUESTIONS

Only rarely is the "essay" question, which you answer in narrative form, used in civil service tests. Civil service tests are usually of the short-answer type. Full instructions for answering these questions will be given to you at the examination. But in case this is your first experience with short-answer questions and separate answer sheets, here is what you need to know:

1) Multiple-choice Questions

Most popular of the short-answer questions is the "multiple choice" or "best answer" question. It can be used, for example, to test for factual knowledge, ability to solve problems or judgment in meeting situations found at work.

A multiple-choice question is normally one of three types—

- It can begin with an incomplete statement followed by several possible endings. You are to find the one ending which *best* completes the statement, although some of the others may not be entirely wrong.
- It can also be a complete statement in the form of a question which is answered by choosing one of the statements listed.

- It can be in the form of a problem – again you select the best answer.

Here is an example of a multiple-choice question with a discussion which should give you some clues as to the method for choosing the right answer:

When an employee has a complaint about his assignment, the action which will *best* help him overcome his difficulty is to

A. discuss his difficulty with his coworkers
B. take the problem to the head of the organization
C. take the problem to the person who gave him the assignment
D. say nothing to anyone about his complaint

In answering this question, you should study each of the choices to find which is best. Consider choice "A" – Certainly an employee may discuss his complaint with fellow employees, but no change or improvement can result, and the complaint remains unresolved. Choice "B" is a poor choice since the head of the organization probably does not know what assignment you have been given, and taking your problem to him is known as "going over the head" of the supervisor. The supervisor, or person who made the assignment, is the person who can clarify it or correct any injustice. Choice "C" is, therefore, correct. To say nothing, as in choice "D," is unwise. Supervisors have and interest in knowing the problems employees are facing, and the employee is seeking a solution to his problem.

2) True/False Questions

The "true/false" or "right/wrong" form of question is sometimes used. Here a complete statement is given. Your job is to decide whether the statement is right or wrong.

SAMPLE: A roaming cell-phone call to a nearby city costs less than a non-roaming call to a distant city.

This statement is wrong, or false, since roaming calls are more expensive.

This is not a complete list of all possible question forms, although most of the others are variations of these common types. You will always get complete directions for answering questions. Be sure you understand *how* to mark your answers – ask questions until you do.

V. RECORDING YOUR ANSWERS

Computer terminals are used more and more today for many different kinds of exams.

For an examination with very few applicants, you may be told to record your answers in the test booklet itself. Separate answer sheets are much more common. If this separate answer sheet is to be scored by machine – and this is often the case – it is highly important that you mark your answers correctly in order to get credit.

An electronic scoring machine is often used in civil service offices because of the speed with which papers can be scored. Machine-scored answer sheets must be marked with a pencil, which will be given to you. This pencil has a high graphite content which responds to the electronic scoring machine. As a matter of fact, stray dots may register as answers, so do not let your pencil rest on the answer sheet while you are pondering the correct answer. Also, if your pencil lead breaks or is otherwise defective, ask for another.

Since the answer sheet will be dropped in a slot in the scoring machine, be careful not to bend the corners or get the paper crumpled.

The answer sheet normally has five vertical columns of numbers, with 30 numbers to a column. These numbers correspond to the question numbers in your test booklet. After each number, going across the page are four or five pairs of dotted lines. These short dotted lines have small letters or numbers above them. The first two pairs may also have a "T" or "F" above the letters. This indicates that the first two pairs only are to be used if the questions are of the true-false type. If the questions are multiple choice, disregard the "T" and "F" and pay attention only to the small letters or numbers.

Answer your questions in the manner of the sample that follows:

32. The largest city in the United States is
    A. Washington, D.C.
    B. New York City
    C. Chicago
    D. Detroit
    E. San Francisco

1) Choose the answer you think is best. (New York City is the largest, so "B" is correct.)
2) Find the row of dotted lines numbered the same as the question you are answering. (Find row number 32)
3) Find the pair of dotted lines corresponding to the answer. (Find the pair of lines under the mark "B.")
4) Make a solid black mark between the dotted lines.

VI. BEFORE THE TEST

Common sense will help you find procedures to follow to get ready for an examination. Too many of us, however, overlook these sensible measures. Indeed, nervousness and fatigue have been found to be the most serious reasons why applicants fail to do their best on civil service tests. Here is a list of reminders:

- Begin your preparation early – Don't wait until the last minute to go scurrying around for books and materials or to find out what the position is all about.
- Prepare continuously – An hour a night for a week is better than an all-night cram session. This has been definitely established. What is more, a night a week for a month will return better dividends than crowding your study into a shorter period of time.
- Locate the place of the exam – You have been sent a notice telling you when and where to report for the examination. If the location is in a different town or otherwise unfamiliar to you, it would be well to inquire the best route and learn something about the building.
- Relax the night before the test – Allow your mind to rest. Do not study at all that night. Plan some mild recreation or diversion; then go to bed early and get a good night's sleep.
- Get up early enough to make a leisurely trip to the place for the test – This way unforeseen events, traffic snarls, unfamiliar buildings, etc. will not upset you.
- Dress comfortably – A written test is not a fashion show. You will be known by number and not by name, so wear something comfortable.

- Leave excess paraphernalia at home – Shopping bags and odd bundles will get in your way. You need bring only the items mentioned in the official notice you received; usually everything you need is provided. Do not bring reference books to the exam. They will only confuse those last minutes and be taken away from you when in the test room.
- Arrive somewhat ahead of time – If because of transportation schedules you must get there very early, bring a newspaper or magazine to take your mind off yourself while waiting.
- Locate the examination room – When you have found the proper room, you will be directed to the seat or part of the room where you will sit. Sometimes you are given a sheet of instructions to read while you are waiting. Do not fill out any forms until you are told to do so; just read them and be prepared.
- Relax and prepare to listen to the instructions
- If you have any physical problem that may keep you from doing your best, be sure to tell the test administrator. If you are sick or in poor health, you really cannot do your best on the exam. You can come back and take the test some other time.

VII. AT THE TEST

The day of the test is here and you have the test booklet in your hand. The temptation to get going is very strong. Caution! There is more to success than knowing the right answers. You must know how to identify your papers and understand variations in the type of short-answer question used in this particular examination. Follow these suggestions for maximum results from your efforts:

1) Cooperate with the monitor

The test administrator has a duty to create a situation in which you can be as much at ease as possible. He will give instructions, tell you when to begin, check to see that you are marking your answer sheet correctly, and so on. He is not there to guard you, although he will see that your competitors do not take unfair advantage. He wants to help you do your best.

2) Listen to all instructions

Don't jump the gun! Wait until you understand all directions. In most civil service tests you get more time than you need to answer the questions. So don't be in a hurry. Read each word of instructions until you clearly understand the meaning. Study the examples, listen to all announcements and follow directions. Ask questions if you do not understand what to do.

3) Identify your papers

Civil service exams are usually identified by number only. You will be assigned a number; you must not put your name on your test papers. Be sure to copy your number correctly. Since more than one exam may be given, copy your exact examination title.

4) Plan your time

Unless you are told that a test is a "speed" or "rate of work" test, speed itself is usually not important. Time enough to answer all the questions will be provided, but this does not mean that you have all day. An overall time limit has been set. Divide the total time (in minutes) by the number of questions to determine the approximate time you have for each question.

5) Do not linger over difficult questions

If you come across a difficult question, mark it with a paper clip (useful to have along) and come back to it when you have been through the booklet. One caution if you do this – be sure to skip a number on your answer sheet as well. Check often to be sure that you have not lost your place and that you are marking in the row numbered the same as the question you are answering.

6) Read the questions

Be sure you know what the question asks! Many capable people are unsuccessful because they failed to *read* the questions correctly.

7) Answer all questions

Unless you have been instructed that a penalty will be deducted for incorrect answers, it is better to guess than to omit a question.

8) Speed tests

It is often better NOT to guess on speed tests. It has been found that on timed tests people are tempted to spend the last few seconds before time is called in marking answers at random – without even reading them – in the hope of picking up a few extra points. To discourage this practice, the instructions may warn you that your score will be "corrected" for guessing. That is, a penalty will be applied. The incorrect answers will be deducted from the correct ones, or some other penalty formula will be used.

9) Review your answers

If you finish before time is called, go back to the questions you guessed or omitted to give them further thought. Review other answers if you have time.

10) Return your test materials

If you are ready to leave before others have finished or time is called, take ALL your materials to the monitor and leave quietly. Never take any test material with you. The monitor can discover whose papers are not complete, and taking a test booklet may be grounds for disqualification.

VIII. EXAMINATION TECHNIQUES

1) Read the general instructions carefully. These are usually printed on the first page of the exam booklet. As a rule, these instructions refer to the timing of the examination; the fact that you should not start work until the signal and must stop work at a signal, etc. If there are any *special* instructions, such as a choice of questions to be answered, make sure that you note this instruction carefully.

2) When you are ready to start work on the examination, that is as soon as the signal has been given, read the instructions to each question booklet, underline any key words or phrases, such as *least*, *best*, *outline*, *describe* and the like. In this way you will tend to answer as requested rather than discover on reviewing your paper that you *listed without describing*, that you selected the *worst* choice rather than the *best* choice, etc.

3) If the examination is of the objective or multiple-choice type – that is, each question will also give a series of possible answers: A, B, C or D, and you are called upon to select the best answer and write the letter next to that answer on your answer paper – it is advisable to start answering each question in turn. There may be anywhere from 50 to 100 such questions in the three or four hours allotted and you can see how much time would be taken if you read through all the questions before beginning to answer any. Furthermore, if you come across a question or group of questions which you know would be difficult to answer, it would undoubtedly affect your handling of all the other questions.

4) If the examination is of the essay type and contains but a few questions, it is a moot point as to whether you should read all the questions before starting to answer any one. Of course, if you are given a choice – say five out of seven and the like – then it is essential to read all the questions so you can eliminate the two that are most difficult. If, however, you are asked to answer all the questions, there may be danger in trying to answer the easiest one first because you may find that you will spend too much time on it. The best technique is to answer the first question, then proceed to the second, etc.

5) Time your answers. Before the exam begins, write down the time it started, then add the time allowed for the examination and write down the time it must be completed, then divide the time available somewhat as follows:
    - If 3-1/2 hours are allowed, that would be 210 minutes. If you have 80 objective-type questions, that would be an average of 2-1/2 minutes per question. Allow yourself no more than 2 minutes per question, or a total of 160 minutes, which will permit about 50 minutes to review.
    - If for the time allotment of 210 minutes there are 7 essay questions to answer, that would average about 30 minutes a question. Give yourself only 25 minutes per question so that you have about 35 minutes to review.

6) The most important instruction is to *read each question* and make sure you know what is wanted. The second most important instruction is to *time yourself properly* so that you answer every question. The third most important instruction is to *answer every question.* Guess if you have to but include something for each question. Remember that you will receive no credit for a blank and will probably receive some credit if you write something in answer to an essay question. If you guess a letter – say "B" for a multiple-choice question – you may have guessed right. If you leave a blank as an answer to a multiple-choice question, the examiners may respect your feelings but it will not add a point to your score. Some exams may penalize you for wrong answers, so in such cases *only*, you may not want to guess unless you have some basis for your answer.

7) Suggestions
    a. Objective-type questions
        1. Examine the question booklet for proper sequence of pages and questions
        2. Read all instructions carefully
        3. Skip any question which seems too difficult; return to it after all other questions have been answered
        4. Apportion your time properly; do not spend too much time on any single question or group of questions

5. Note and underline key words – *all, most, fewest, least, best, worst, same, opposite,* etc.
6. Pay particular attention to negatives
7. Note unusual option, e.g., unduly long, short, complex, different or similar in content to the body of the question
8. Observe the use of "hedging" words – *probably, may, most likely,* etc.
9. Make sure that your answer is put next to the same number as the question
10. Do not second-guess unless you have good reason to believe the second answer is definitely more correct
11. Cross out original answer if you decide another answer is more accurate; do not erase until you are ready to hand your paper in
12. Answer all questions; guess unless instructed otherwise
13. Leave time for review

b. Essay questions
   1. Read each question carefully
   2. Determine exactly what is wanted. Underline key words or phrases.
   3. Decide on outline or paragraph answer
   4. Include many different points and elements unless asked to develop any one or two points or elements
   5. Show impartiality by giving pros and cons unless directed to select one side only
   6. Make and write down any assumptions you find necessary to answer the questions
   7. Watch your English, grammar, punctuation and choice of words
   8. Time your answers; don't crowd material

8) Answering the essay question

Most essay questions can be answered by framing the specific response around several key words or ideas. Here are a few such key words or ideas:

M's: manpower, materials, methods, money, management
P's: purpose, program, policy, plan, procedure, practice, problems, pitfalls, personnel, public relations

a. Six basic steps in handling problems:
   1. Preliminary plan and background development
   2. Collect information, data and facts
   3. Analyze and interpret information, data and facts
   4. Analyze and develop solutions as well as make recommendations
   5. Prepare report and sell recommendations
   6. Install recommendations and follow up effectiveness

b. Pitfalls to avoid
   1. *Taking things for granted* – A statement of the situation does not necessarily imply that each of the elements is necessarily true; for example, a complaint may be invalid and biased so that all that can be taken for granted is that a complaint has been registered

2. *Considering only one side of a situation* – Wherever possible, indicate several alternatives and then point out the reasons you selected the best one
3. *Failing to indicate follow up* – Whenever your answer indicates action on your part, make certain that you will take proper follow-up action to see how successful your recommendations, procedures or actions turn out to be
4. *Taking too long in answering any single question* – Remember to time your answers properly

IX. AFTER THE TEST

Scoring procedures differ in detail among civil service jurisdictions although the general principles are the same. Whether the papers are hand-scored or graded by machine we have described, they are nearly always graded by number. That is, the person who marks the paper knows only the number – never the name – of the applicant. Not until all the papers have been graded will they be matched with names. If other tests, such as training and experience or oral interview ratings have been given, scores will be combined. Different parts of the examination usually have different weights. For example, the written test might count 60 percent of the final grade, and a rating of training and experience 40 percent. In many jurisdictions, veterans will have a certain number of points added to their grades.

After the final grade has been determined, the names are placed in grade order and an eligible list is established. There are various methods for resolving ties between those who get the same final grade – probably the most common is to place first the name of the person whose application was received first. Job offers are made from the eligible list in the order the names appear on it. You will be notified of your grade and your rank as soon as all these computations have been made. This will be done as rapidly as possible.

People who are found to meet the requirements in the announcement are called "eligibles." Their names are put on a list of eligible candidates. An eligible's chances of getting a job depend on how high he stands on this list and how fast agencies are filling jobs from the list.

When a job is to be filled from a list of eligibles, the agency asks for the names of people on the list of eligibles for that job. When the civil service commission receives this request, it sends to the agency the names of the three people highest on this list. Or, if the job to be filled has specialized requirements, the office sends the agency the names of the top three persons who meet these requirements from the general list.

The appointing officer makes a choice from among the three people whose names were sent to him. If the selected person accepts the appointment, the names of the others are put back on the list to be considered for future openings.

That is the rule in hiring from all kinds of eligible lists, whether they are for typist, carpenter, chemist, or something else. For every vacancy, the appointing officer has his choice of any one of the top three eligibles on the list. This explains why the person whose name is on top of the list sometimes does not get an appointment when some of the persons lower on the list do. If the appointing officer chooses the second or third eligible, the No. 1 eligible does not get a job at once, but stays on the list until he is appointed or the list is terminated.

X. HOW TO PASS THE INTERVIEW TEST

The examination for which you applied requires an oral interview test. You have already taken the written test and you are now being called for the interview test – the final part of the formal examination.

You may think that it is not possible to prepare for an interview test and that there are no procedures to follow during an interview. Our purpose is to point out some things you can do in advance that will help you and some good rules to follow and pitfalls to avoid while you are being interviewed.

What is an interview supposed to test?

The written examination is designed to test the technical knowledge and competence of the candidate; the oral is designed to evaluate intangible qualities, not readily measured otherwise, and to establish a list showing the relative fitness of each candidate – as measured against his competitors – for the position sought. Scoring is not on the basis of "right" and "wrong," but on a sliding scale of values ranging from "not passable" to "outstanding." As a matter of fact, it is possible to achieve a relatively low score without a single "incorrect" answer because of evident weakness in the qualities being measured.

Occasionally, an examination may consist entirely of an oral test – either an individual or a group oral. In such cases, information is sought concerning the technical knowledges and abilities of the candidate, since there has been no written examination for this purpose. More commonly, however, an oral test is used to supplement a written examination.

Who conducts interviews?

The composition of oral boards varies among different jurisdictions. In nearly all, a representative of the personnel department serves as chairman. One of the members of the board may be a representative of the department in which the candidate would work. In some cases, "outside experts" are used, and, frequently, a businessman or some other representative of the general public is asked to serve. Labor and management or other special groups may be represented. The aim is to secure the services of experts in the appropriate field.

However the board is composed, it is a good idea (and not at all improper or unethical) to ascertain in advance of the interview who the members are and what groups they represent. When you are introduced to them, you will have some idea of their backgrounds and interests, and at least you will not stutter and stammer over their names.

What should be done before the interview?

While knowledge about the board members is useful and takes some of the surprise element out of the interview, there is other preparation which is more substantive. It *is* possible to prepare for an oral interview – in several ways:

1) Keep a copy of your application and review it carefully before the interview

This may be the only document before the oral board, and the starting point of the interview. Know what education and experience you have listed there, and the sequence and dates of all of it. Sometimes the board will ask you to review the highlights of your experience for them; you should not have to hem and haw doing it.

2) Study the class specification and the examination announcement

Usually, the oral board has one or both of these to guide them. The qualities, characteristics or knowledges required by the position sought are stated in these documents. They offer valuable clues as to the nature of the oral interview. For example, if the job involves supervisory responsibilities, the announcement will usually indicate that knowledge of modern supervisory methods and the qualifications of the candidate as a supervisor will be tested. If so, you can expect such questions, frequently in the form of a hypothetical situation which you are expected to solve. NEVER go into an oral without knowledge of the duties and responsibilities of the job you seek.

3) Think through each qualification required

Try to visualize the kind of questions you would ask if you were a board member. How well could you answer them? Try especially to appraise your own knowledge and background in each area, *measured against the job sought*, and identify any areas in which you are weak. Be critical and realistic – do not flatter yourself.

4) Do some general reading in areas in which you feel you may be weak

For example, if the job involves supervision and your past experience has NOT, some general reading in supervisory methods and practices, particularly in the field of human relations, might be useful. Do NOT study agency procedures or detailed manuals. The oral board will be testing your understanding and capacity, not your memory.

5) Get a good night's sleep and watch your general health and mental attitude

You will want a clear head at the interview. Take care of a cold or any other minor ailment, and of course, no hangovers.

What should be done on the day of the interview?

Now comes the day of the interview itself. Give yourself plenty of time to get there. Plan to arrive somewhat ahead of the scheduled time, particularly if your appointment is in the fore part of the day. If a previous candidate fails to appear, the board might be ready for you a bit early. By early afternoon an oral board is almost invariably behind schedule if there are many candidates, and you may have to wait. Take along a book or magazine to read, or your application to review, but leave any extraneous material in the waiting room when you go in for your interview. In any event, relax and compose yourself.

The matter of dress is important. The board is forming impressions about you – from your experience, your manners, your attitude, and your appearance. Give your personal appearance careful attention. Dress your best, but not your flashiest. Choose conservative, appropriate clothing, and be sure it is immaculate. This is a business interview, and your appearance should indicate that you regard it as such. Besides, being well groomed and properly dressed will help boost your confidence.

Sooner or later, someone will call your name and escort you into the interview room. *This is it.* From here on you are on your own. It is too late for any more preparation. But remember, you asked for this opportunity to prove your fitness, and you are here because your request was granted.

What happens when you go in?

The usual sequence of events will be as follows: The clerk (who is often the board stenographer) will introduce you to the chairman of the oral board, who will introduce you to the other members of the board. Acknowledge the introductions before you sit down. Do not be surprised if you find a microphone facing you or a stenotypist sitting by. Oral interviews are usually recorded in the event of an appeal or other review.

Usually the chairman of the board will open the interview by reviewing the highlights of your education and work experience from your application – primarily for the benefit of the other members of the board, as well as to get the material into the record. Do not interrupt or comment unless there is an error or significant misinterpretation; if that is the case, do not hesitate. But do not quibble about insignificant matters. Also, he will usually ask you some question about your education, experience or your present job – partly to get you to start talking and to establish the interviewing "rapport." He may start the actual questioning, or turn it over to one of the other members. Frequently, each member undertakes the questioning on a particular area, one in which he is perhaps most competent, so you can expect each member to participate in the examination. Because time is limited, you may also expect some rather abrupt switches in the direction the questioning takes, so do not be upset by it. Normally, a board member will not pursue a single line of questioning unless he discovers a particular strength or weakness.

After each member has participated, the chairman will usually ask whether any member has any further questions, then will ask you if you have anything you wish to add. Unless you are expecting this question, it may floor you. Worse, it may start you off on an extended, extemporaneous speech. The board is not usually seeking more information. The question is principally to offer you a last opportunity to present further qualifications or to indicate that you have nothing to add. So, if you feel that a significant qualification or characteristic has been overlooked, it is proper to point it out in a sentence or so. Do not compliment the board on the thoroughness of their examination – they have been sketchy, and you know it. If you wish, merely say, "No thank you, I have nothing further to add." This is a point where you can "talk yourself out" of a good impression or fail to present an important bit of information. Remember, *you close the interview yourself.*

The chairman will then say, "That is all, Mr. _______, thank you." Do not be startled; the interview is over, and quicker than you think. Thank him, gather your belongings and take your leave. Save your sigh of relief for the other side of the door.

How to put your best foot forward

Throughout this entire process, you may feel that the board individually and collectively is trying to pierce your defenses, seek out your hidden weaknesses and embarrass and confuse you. Actually, this is not true. They are obliged to make an appraisal of your qualifications for the job you are seeking, and they want to see you in your best light. Remember, they must interview all candidates and a non-cooperative candidate may become a failure in spite of their best efforts to bring out his qualifications. Here are 15 suggestions that will help you:

1) Be natural – Keep your attitude confident, not cocky

If you are not confident that you can do the job, do not expect the board to be. Do not apologize for your weaknesses, try to bring out your strong points. The board is interested in a positive, not negative, presentation. Cockiness will antagonize any board member and make him wonder if you are covering up a weakness by a false show of strength.

2) Get comfortable, but don't lounge or sprawl

Sit erectly but not stiffly. A careless posture may lead the board to conclude that you are careless in other things, or at least that you are not impressed by the importance of the occasion. Either conclusion is natural, even if incorrect. Do not fuss with your clothing, a pencil or an ashtray. Your hands may occasionally be useful to emphasize a point; do not let them become a point of distraction.

3) Do not wisecrack or make small talk

This is a serious situation, and your attitude should show that you consider it as such. Further, the time of the board is limited – they do not want to waste it, and neither should you.

4) Do not exaggerate your experience or abilities

In the first place, from information in the application or other interviews and sources, the board may know more about you than you think. Secondly, you probably will not get away with it. An experienced board is rather adept at spotting such a situation, so do not take the chance.

5) If you know a board member, do not make a point of it, yet do not hide it

Certainly you are not fooling him, and probably not the other members of the board. Do not try to take advantage of your acquaintanceship – it will probably do you little good.

6) Do not dominate the interview

Let the board do that. They will give you the clues – do not assume that you have to do all the talking. Realize that the board has a number of questions to ask you, and do not try to take up all the interview time by showing off your extensive knowledge of the answer to the first one.

7) Be attentive

You only have 20 minutes or so, and you should keep your attention at its sharpest throughout. When a member is addressing a problem or question to you, give him your undivided attention. Address your reply principally to him, but do not exclude the other board members.

8) Do not interrupt

A board member may be stating a problem for you to analyze. He will ask you a question when the time comes. Let him state the problem, and wait for the question.

9) Make sure you understand the question

Do not try to answer until you are sure what the question is. If it is not clear, restate it in your own words or ask the board member to clarify it for you. However, do not haggle about minor elements.

10) Reply promptly but not hastily

A common entry on oral board rating sheets is "candidate responded readily," or "candidate hesitated in replies." Respond as promptly and quickly as you can, but do not jump to a hasty, ill-considered answer.

11) Do not be peremptory in your answers

A brief answer is proper – but do not fire your answer back. That is a losing game from your point of view. The board member can probably ask questions much faster than you can answer them.

12) Do not try to create the answer you think the board member wants

He is interested in what kind of mind you have and how it works – not in playing games. Furthermore, he can usually spot this practice and will actually grade you down on it.

13) Do not switch sides in your reply merely to agree with a board member

Frequently, a member will take a contrary position merely to draw you out and to see if you are willing and able to defend your point of view. Do not start a debate, yet do not surrender a good position. If a position is worth taking, it is worth defending.

14) Do not be afraid to admit an error in judgment if you are shown to be wrong

The board knows that you are forced to reply without any opportunity for careful consideration. Your answer may be demonstrably wrong. If so, admit it and get on with the interview.

15) Do not dwell at length on your present job

The opening question may relate to your present assignment. Answer the question but do not go into an extended discussion. You are being examined for a *new* job, not your present one. As a matter of fact, try to phrase ALL your answers in terms of the job for which you are being examined.

Basis of Rating

Probably you will forget most of these "do's" and "don'ts" when you walk into the oral interview room. Even remembering them all will not ensure you a passing grade. Perhaps you did not have the qualifications in the first place. But remembering them will help you to put your best foot forward, without treading on the toes of the board members.

Rumor and popular opinion to the contrary notwithstanding, an oral board wants you to make the best appearance possible. They know you are under pressure – but they also want to see how you respond to it as a guide to what your reaction would be under the pressures of the job you seek. They will be influenced by the degree of poise you display, the personal traits you show and the manner in which you respond.

ABOUT THIS BOOK

This book contains tests divided into Examination Sections. Go through each test, answering every question in the margin. We have also attached a sample answer sheet at the back of the book that can be removed and used. At the end of each test look at the answer key and check your answers. On the ones you got wrong, look at the right answer choice and learn. Do not fill in the answers first. Do not memorize the questions and answers, but understand the answer and principles involved. On your test, the questions will likely be different from the samples. Questions are changed and new ones added. If you understand these past questions you should have success with any changes that arise. Tests may consist of several types of questions. We have additional books on each subject should more study be advisable or necessary for you. Finally, the more you study, the better prepared you will be. This book is intended to be the last thing you study before you walk into the examination room. Prior study of relevant texts is also recommended. NLC publishes some of these in our Fundamental Series. Knowledge and good sense are important factors in passing your exam. Good luck also helps. So now study this Passbook, absorb the material contained within and take that knowledge into the examination. Then do your best to pass that exam.

EXAMINATION SECTION

EXAMINATION SECTION

TEST 1

DIRECTIONS: Each question or incomplete statement is followed by several suggested answers or completions. Select the one that BEST answers the question or completes the statement. *PRINT THE LETTER OF THE CORRECT ANSWER IN THE SPACE AT THE RIGHT.*

1. It is often desirable for an administrator to consult, during the planning process, the persons to be affected by those plans. 1.____
Of the following, the MAJOR justification for such consultation is that it recognizes the
   A. fact that participating in horizontal planning is almost always more effective than participating in vertical planning
   B. principle of participation and the need for a sense of belonging as a means of decreasing resistance and developing support
   C. principle that lower-level administrators normally are more likely than higher-level administrators to emphasize longer-range goals
   D. fact that final responsibility for the approval of plans should be placed in committees not individuals

2. In evaluating performance and, if necessary, correcting what is being done to assure attainment of results according to plan, it is GENERALLY best for the administrator to do which one of the following? 2.____
   A. Make a continual effort to increase the number of written control reports prepared
   B. Thoroughly investigate in equal detail all possible deviations indicated by comparison of performance to expectation
   C. Decentralize, within an operating unit or division, the responsibility for correcting deviations
   D. Concentrate on the exceptions, or outstanding variations, from the expected results or standards

3. Generally, changes in the ways in which the supervisors and employees in an organization do things are MORE likely to be welcomed by them when the changes 3.____
   A. threaten the security of the supervisors than when they do not
   B. are inaugurated after prior change has been assimilated than when they are inaugurated before other major changes have been assimilated
   C. follow a series of failures in changes when they follow a series of successful changes
   D. are dictated by personal order rather than when they result from an application of previously established impersonal principles

4. For sound organization relationships, of the following, it is generally MOST desirable that 4.____
   A. authority and responsibility be segregated from each other, in order to facilitate control
   B. the authority of a manager should be commensurate with his responsibility, and vice versa
   C. authority be defined as the obligation of an individual to carry out assigned activities to the best of his or her ability
   D. clear recognition be given to the fact that delegation of authority benefits only the manager who delegates it

5. In utilizing a checklist of questions for general managerial planning, which one of the following generally is the FIRST question to be asked and answered? 5.____
   A. Where will it take place?
   B. How will it be done?
   C. Why must it be done?
   D. Who will do it?

6. Of the following, it is USUALLY best to set administrative objectives so that they are 6.____
   A. at a level that is unattainable, so that administrators will continually be strongly motivated
   B. at a level that is attainable, but requires some stretching and reaching by administrators trying to attain them
   C. stated in qualitative rather than quantitative terms whenever a choice between the two is possible
   D. stated in a general and unstructured manner, to permit each administrator maximum freedom in interpreting them

7. In selecting from among administrative alternatives, three general bases for decisions are open to the manager – experience, experimentation, and research and analysis. Of the following, the best argument AGAINST primary reliance upon experimentation as the method of evaluating administrative alternatives is that experimentation is 7.____
   A. generally the most expensive of the three techniques
   B. almost always legally prohibited in procedural matters
   C. possible only in areas where results may be easily duplicated by other experimenters at any time
   D. an approach that requires information on scientific method seldom available to administrators

8. The administrator who utilizes the techniques of operations research, linear programming and simulation in making an administrative decision should MOST appropriately be considered to be using the techniques of ______ analysis. 8.____
   A. intuitive
   B. quantitative
   C. nonmathematical
   D. qualitative

9. When an additional organizational level is added within a department, that department has MOST directly manifested 9.____
   A. horizontal growth B. horizontal shrinkage
   C. vertical growth D. vertical shrinkage

10. Of the following, the one which GENERALLY is the most intangible planning factor is 10.____
   A. budget dollars allocated to a function
   B. square feet of space for office use
   C. number of personnel in various clerical titles
   D. emotional impact of a proposed personnel policy among employees

11. Departmentation by function is the same as, or most similar to, departmentation by 11.____
   A. equipment B. clientele
   C. territory D. activity

12. Such verifiable factors as turnover, absenteeism or volume of grievances would generally BEST assist in measuring the effectiveness of a program to improve 12.____
   A. forms control B. employee morale
   C. linear programming D. executive creativity

13. An organization increases the number of subordinates reporting to a manager up to the point where incremental savings in costs, better communication and morale, and other factors equal incremental losses in effectiveness of control, direction and similar factors. This action MOST specifically employs the technique of 13.____
   A. role playing
   B. queuing theory
   C. marginal analysis
   D. capital standards analysis

14. The term *computer hardware* is MOST likely to refer to 14.____
   A. machines and equipment
   B. Ethernet and USB cables
   C. training manuals
   D. word processing and spreadsheet programs

15. Determining what is being accomplished, that is, evaluating the performance and, if necessary, applying corrective measures so that performance takes place according to plans is MOST appropriately called management 15.____
   A. actuating B. planning
   C. controlling D. motivating

16. Of the following, the BEST overall technique for choosing from among several alternative public programs proposed to try to achieve the same broad objective generally is ______ analysis. 16.____
    A. random-sample
    B. input
    C. cost-effectiveness
    D. output

17. When the success of a plan in achieving specific program objectives is measured against that plan's costs, the measure obtained is most directly that of the plan's 17.____
    A. pervasiveness
    B. control potential
    C. primacy
    D. efficiency

18. Generally, the degree to which an organization's planning will be coordinated varies MOST directly with the degree to which 18.____
    A. the individuals charged with executing plans are better compensated than those charged with developing and evaluating plans
    B. the individuals charged with planning understand and agree to utilize consistent planning premises
    C. a large number of position classification titles have been established for those individuals charged with organizational planning functions
    D. subordinate unit objectives are allowed to control the overall objectives of the departments of which such subordinate units are a part

19. The responsibility for specific types of decisions generally is BEST delegated to 19.____
    A. the highest organizational level at which there is an individual possessing the ability, desire, impartiality and access to relevant information needed to make these decisions
    B. the lowest organizational level at which there is an individual possessing the ability, desire, impartiality and access to relevant information needed to make these decisions
    C. a group of executives, rather than a single executive, if these decisions deal with an emergency
    D. the organizational level midway between that which will have to carry out these decisions and that which will have to authorize the resources for their implementation

20. The process of managing by objectives is MOST likely to lead to a situation in which the 20.____
    A. goal accomplishment objectives of managers tend to have a longer timespan as one goes lower down the line in an organization
    B. establishment of quantitative goals for staff positions is generally easier than the establishment of quantitative goals for line positions
    C. development of objectives requires the manager to think of the way he will accomplish given results, and of the organization, personnel and resources that he will need
    D. superiors normally develop and finally approve detailed goals for subordinates without any prior consultation with either those subordinates or with the top-level executives responsible for the longer-run objectives of the organization

21. As used with respect to decision making, the application of scientific method to the study of alternatives in a problem situation, with a view to providing a quantitative basis for arriving at an optimum solution in terms of the goals sought is MOST appropriately called 21.____
    A. simple number departmentation
    B. geographic decentralization
    C. operations research
    D. trait rating

22. Assume that a bureau head proposes that final responsibility and authority for all planning within the bureau is to be delegated to one employee who is to be paid at the level of an assistant division head in that bureau. 22.____
    Of the following, the MOST appropriate comment about this proposal is that it's
    A. *improper*, mainly because planning does not call for someone at such a high level
    B. *improper*, mainly because responsibility for a basic management function such as planning may not properly be delegated as proposed
    C. *proper*, mainly because ultimate responsibility for all bureau planning is best placed as proposed
    D. *proper*, mainly because every well-managed bureau should have a full-time planning officer

23. Of the following, the MOST important reason that participation has motivating effects is generally that it gives to the individual participating 23.____
    A. a recognition of his or her desire to feel important and to contribute to achievement of worthwhile goals
    B. an opportunity to participate in work that is beyond the scope of the class specification for his or her title
    C. a secure knowledge that his or her organization's top leadership is as efficient as possible considering all major circumstances
    D. the additional information likely to be crucial to his or her promotion

24. Of the following, the MOST essential characteristic of an effective employee suggestion system is that 24.____
    A. suggestions be submitted upward through the chain of command
    B. suggestions be acted upon promptly so that employees may be promptly informed of what happens to their submitted suggestions
    C. suggesters be required to sign their names on the material sent to the actual evaluators for evaluation
    D. suggesters receive at least 25% of the agency's savings during the first two years after their suggestions have been accepted and put into effect by the agency

25. Two organizations have the same basic objectives and the same total number of employees. The span of authority of each intermediate manager is narrower in one organization than it is in the other. It is MOST likely that the organization in which each intermediate manager has a narrower span of authority will have 25.____
    A. fewer intermediate managers
    B. more organizational levels
    C. more managers reporting to a larger number of intermediate supervisors
    D. more characteristics of a *flat* organizational structure

---

KEY (CORRECT ANSWERS)

1.	B	11.	D
2.	D	12.	B
3.	B	13.	C
4.	B	14.	A
5.	C	15.	C
6.	B	16.	C
7.	A	17.	D
8.	B	18.	B
9.	C	19.	B
10.	D	20.	C

21. C
22. B
23. A
24. B
25. B

TEST 2

DIRECTIONS: Each question or incomplete statement is followed by several suggested answers or completions. Select the one that BEST answers the question or completes the statement. *PRINT THE LETTER OF THE CORRECT ANSWER IN THE SPACE AT THE RIGHT.*

1. Which one of the following BEST expresses the essence of the merit idea or system in public employment? 1.____
   A. A person's worth to the organization—the merit of his or her attributes and capacities—is the governing factor in his or her selection, assignment, pay, recognition, advancement and retention
   B. Written tests of the objective type are the only fair way to select on a merit basis from among candidates for open-competitive appointment to positions within the merit system
   C. Employees who have qualified for civil service positions shall have lifetime tenure during good behavior in those positions regardless of changes in public programs
   D. Periodic examinations with set date limits within which all persons desiring to demonstrate their merit may apply, shall be publicly advertised and held for all promotional titles

2. Of the following, the promotion selection policy generally considered MOST antithetical to the merit concept is the promotion selection policy which 2.____
   A. is based solely on objective tests of competence
   B. is based solely on seniority
   C. may require a manager to lose his or her best employee to another part of the organization
   D. permits operating managers collectively to play a significant role in promotion decisions

3. Of the following, the problems encountered by government establishments which are MOST likely to make extensive delegation of authority difficult to effectuate tend to be problems of 3.____
   A. accountability and ensuring uniform administration
   B. line and staff relationships within field offices
   C. generally employee opposition to such delegation of authority and to the subsequent record-keeping activities
   D. use of the management-by-objectives approach

4. The major decisions as to which jobs shall be created and who shall carry which responsibilities should GENERALLY be made by 4.____
   A. budgetary advisers
   B. line managers
   C. classification specialists
   D. peer-level rating committees

5. The ultimate controlling factor in structuring positions in the public service, MOST generally, should be the 5.____
   A. possibility of providing upgrading for highly productive employees
   B. collective bargaining demands initially made by established public employee unions
   C. positive motivational effects upon productivity resulting from an inverted pyramid job structure
   D. effectiveness of the structuring in serving the mission of the organization

6. Of the following, the most usual reason for unsatisfactory line-staff relationships is 6.____
   A. inept use of the abilities of staff personnel by line management
   B. the higher salaries paid to line officials
   C. excessive consultation between line officials and staff officials at the same organizational level
   D. a feeling among the staff members that only lower-level line members appreciate their work

7. Generally, an employee receiving new information from a fellow employee is MOST likely to 7.____
   A. forget the new information if it is consistent with his or her existing beliefs much more easily than he or she forgets the new information if it is inconsistent with existing beliefs
   B. accept the validity of the new information if it is consistent with his or her existing beliefs more readily than he or she accepts the validity of the new information if it is inconsistent with existing beliefs
   C. have a less accurate memory of the new information if it is consistent with his or her existing beliefs than he or she has of the new information if it is inconsistent with existing beliefs
   D. ignore the new information if it is consistent with his or her existing beliefs more often than he or she ignores the new information if it is inconsistent with existing beliefs

8. Virtually all of us use this principle in our human communications – perhaps without realizing it. In casual conversations, we are alert for cues to whether we are understood (e.g., attentive nods from the other person). Similarly, an instructor is always interested in reactions among those to whom he is giving instruction. The effective administrator is equally conscious of the need to determine his or her subordinates' reactions to what he or she is trying to communicate. 8.____
   The principle referred to in the above selection is MOST appropriately called
   A. cognitive dissonance
   B. feedback
   C. negative reinforcement
   D. noise transmission

9. Of the following, the PRINCIPAL function of an *ombudsman* generally is to 9.____
   A. review departmental requests for new data processing equipment so as to reduce duplication
   B. receive and investigate complaints from citizens who are displeased with the actions or non-actions of administrative officials and try to effectuate warranted remedies
   C. review proposed departmental reorganizations in order to advise the chief executive whether or not they are in accordance with the latest principles of proper management structuring
   D. presiding over courts of the judiciary convened to try *sitting* judges

10. Of the following, the MOST valid reason for recruiting an intermediate-level administrator from outside an agency, rather than from within the agency, normally is to 10.____
   A. improve the public image of the agency as a desirable place in which to be employed
   B. reduce the number of potential administrators who must be evaluated prior to filling the position
   C. minimize the morale problems arising from frequent internal staff upgradings
   D. obtain fresh ideas and a fresh viewpoint on agency problems

11. A MAJOR research finding regarding employee absenteeism is that 11.____
   A. absenteeism is likely to be higher on hot days
   B male employees tend to be absent more than female employees
   C. the way an employee is treated as a definite bearing on absenteeism
   D. the distance employees have to travel is one of the most important factors in absenteeism

12. Of the following, the supervisory behavior that is of GREATEST benefit to the organization is exhibited by supervisors who 12.____
   A. are strict with subordinates about following rules and regulations
   B. encourage subordinates to be interested in the work
   C. are willing to assist with subordinates' work on most occasions
   D. get the most done with available staff and resources

13. The management of time is one of the critical aspects of any supervisor's performance.
Therefore, in evaluating a subordinate from the viewpoint of how he manages time, a supervisor should rate HIGHEST the subordinate who 13.____
A. concentrates on each task as he undertakes it
B. performs at a standard and predictable pace under all circumstances
C. takes shortened lunch periods when he is busy
D. tries to do two things simultaneously

14. A MAJOR research finding regarding employee absenteeism is that 14.____
A. absenteeism is likely to be higher on hot days
B male employees tend to be absent more than female employees
C. the way an employee is treated as a definite bearing on absenteeism
D. the distance employees have to travel is one of the most important factors in absenteeism

15. Of the following, the supervisory behavior that is of GREATEST benefit to the organization is exhibited by supervisors who 15.____
A. are strict with subordinates about following rules and regulations
B. encourage subordinates to be interested in the work
C. are willing to assist with subordinates' work on most occasions
D. get the most done with available staff and resources

16. In order to maintain a proper relationship with a worker who is assigned to staff rather than line functions, a line supervisor should 16.____
A. accept all recommendations of the staff worker
B. include the staff worker in the conferences called by the supervisor for his subordinates
C. keep the staff worker informed of developments in the area of his staff assignment
D. require that the staff worker's recommendations be communicated to the supervisor through the supervisor's own superior

17. Of the following, the GREATEST disadvantage of placing a worker in a staff position under the direct supervision of the supervisor whom he advises is the possibility that the 17.____
A. staff worker will tend to be insubordinate because of a feeling of superiority over the supervisor
B. staff worker will tend to give advice of the type which the supervisor wants to hear or finds acceptable
C. supervisor will tend to be mistrustful of the advice of a worker of subordinate rank
D. supervisor will tend to derive little benefit from the advice because to supervise properly he should know at least as much as his subordinate

18. One factor which might be given consideration in deciding upon the optimum span of control of a supervisor over his immediate subordinates is the position of the supervisor in the hierarchy of the organization. 18.____
It is generally considered proper that the number of subordinates immediately supervised by a higher, upper echelon, supervisor
    A. is unrelated to and tends to form no pattern with the number of supervised by lower level supervisors
    B. should be about the same as the number supervised by a lower level supervisor
    C. should be larger than the number supervised by a lower level supervisor
    D. should be smaller than the number supervised by a lower level supervisor

19. Assume that you are a supervisor and have been assigned to assist the head of a large agency unit. He asks you to prepare a simple, functional organization chart of the unit. 19.____
Such a chart would be USEFUL for
    A. favorably impressing members of the public with the important nature of the agency's work
    B. graphically presenting staff relationships which may indicate previously unknown duplications, overlaps, and gaps in job duties
    C. motivating all employees toward better performance because they will have a better understanding of job procedures
    D. subtly and inoffensively making known to the staff in the unit that you are now in a position of responsibility

20. In some large organizations, management's traditional means of learning about employee dissatisfaction has been in the *open door policy*. 20.____
This policy USUALLY means that
    A. management lets it be known that a management representative is generally available to discuss employees' questions, suggestions, and complaints
    B. management sets up an informal employee organization to establish a democratic procedure for orderly representation of employees
    C. employees are encouraged to attempt to resolve dissatisfactions at the lowest possible level of authority
    D. employees are provided with an address or box so that they may safely and anonymously register complaints

KEY (CORRECT ANSWERS)

1.	B	11.	A
2.	A	12.	D
3.	D	13.	A
4.	B	14.	C
5.	A	15.	D
6.	A	16.	C
7.	B	17.	B
8.	B	18.	D
9.	D	19.	B
10.	C	20.	A

EXAMINATION SECTION

TEST 1

DIRECTIONS: Each question or incomplete statement is followed by several suggested answers or completions. Select the one that BEST answers the question or completes the statement. *PRINT THE LETTER OF THE CORRECT ANSWER IN THE SPACE AT THE RIGHT.*

1. The new head of a central filing unit, after studying a procedure in use, decided that it was unsatisfactory. He thereupon drew up an entirely new procedure which made no use of and ignored the existing procedure. 1.____
This plan of action is, in general,
   A. *satisfactory*; a new broom sweeps clean
   B. *unsatisfactory*; any plan should use available resources to the utmost before resorting to new creation
   C. *satisfactory*; in general, use of part of an old procedure and part of a new procedure results sin an unworkable patchwork arrangement
   D. *unsatisfactory*; before deciding that the existing procedure was unusable, he should have requested that an independent, unbiased agency study the problem
   E. *satisfactory*; it is usually less time consuming to construct a new plan than to remedy an old one

2. Assume that you have broken a complex job into simpler and smaller components. 2.____
After you have assigned a component to each employee, should you proceed to teach each employee a number of alternative methods for doing his job?
   A. *yes*; the more methods for performing a job an employee knows, the more chance there is that he will choose the one best suited to his abilities
   B. *No*; experienced employees should be permitted to decide how to perform the jobs assigned to them
   C. *Yes*; if several different methods are available, a desirable flexibility of operation results
   D. *No*; a single method for each job should be decided upon and taught
   E. *Yes*; the employees will have greater interest in their jobs

3. Assume that you are the head of a major staff unit and that a line unit has requested from your unit a special report to be completed in one day. After reviewing the request, you decide that much tie would be saved if two items which you know are superfluous are omitted from the report. You discuss the matter with the head of the other unit and he still insists that the two items are essential for his purposes. 3.____
The one of the following actions which you should take at this stage is to
   A. plan to complete the report, including the two items, as expeditiously as possible
   B. write a memorandum to the department head giving both opinions fairly and asking for a decision

C. plan to complete the report without the two items, as expeditiously as possible
D. devise a plan for preparing the report without the two items which will permit you to add them later if they prove necessary although some time may be lost
E. again review the report with the line unit showing them why the two items are unnecessary

4. The one of the following functions of a supervisor which can be MOST successfully delegated is 4.____
A. responsibility for accomplishing the unit's mission
B. handling discipline
C. checking completed work
D. reporting to the bureau chief
E. placing subordinates in the proper job

5. It is a standard operating procedure in an office which receives several thousand forms each week to have the file on clerk accumulate a week's receipts before filing them. The forms will not be examined for a period of one month after receipt. 5.____
In comparison with daily filing, this procedure is, in general,
A. *less satisfactory*; it keeps the files unnecessarily incomplete
B. *more satisfactory*; it tends to reduce filing time
C. *less satisfactory*; all information should be placed in a safe storage place as soon as possible
D. *more satisfactory*; it tends to eliminate the prefiling period
E. *less satisfactory*; it tends to build up an unnecessary period

6. Some organizations attempt to keep a constant backlog of work. 6.____
This procedure is usually
A. *undesirable*; reports are not ready when they are needed
B. *desirable*; it tends to insure continuity of work flow
C. *undesirable*; production records are too difficult to keep
D. *desirable*; it tends to keep the employees under constant pressure
E. *undesirable*; it tends to keep the employees under constant pressure

7. The first few times a procedure is carried through, a close check should be kept of all work times. 7.____
The PRIMARY reason for this is to
A. be able to present a clear picture of the situation
B. determine if the employees understand the procedure
C. evaluate the efficiency which may have been presented by the new procedure
D. determine the efficiency of the employees
E. permit revision of schedules

8. The one of the following pieces of information which is of LEAST importance in setting up the schedule for a given job is the time 8.____
   A. which is required to perform each component of the job
   B. when the source material will be available
   C. the job will take under adverse conditions
   D. by which the job must be completed
   E employees will be available

9. Every employee should have a thorough knowledge of the organization of which he is a part. 9.____
   Of the following, the BEST justification for the above opinion is that
   A. the feeling of being a member of a team develops a responsible attitude toward one's everyday duties
   B. in an emergency, an employee may be called upon to perform duties other than his own
   C. the intricate details of an organization as complicated as a city department cannot easily be reduced to an organization chart
   D. an understanding of the different specialized units in an organization is often necessary to achieve the organization's given objective
   E. many city jobs are technical; thus, each employee should be trained to have more than a single narrow skill

10. The one of the following which is NOT a good rule in administering discipline is for you as a supervisor to 10.____
   A. reprimand the employee in private even though the fault was committed before others
   B. allow the employee a chance to reply to your criticism if he wishes
   C. be as specific as possible in criticizing the employee for his faults
   D. be sure you have all the facts before you reprimand an employee for an error he has committed
   E. allow an extended period to elapse after an error has been committed before reprimanding an employee

11. After you have submitted your annual evaluations of the work of your subordinates, one of them whose work has not been satisfactory complains to you that your evaluation was unjustified. 11.____
   For you to avoid discussing the evaluation but to point out two or three specific instances where the employee's work was below standard is
   A. *desirable*; an employee should be told what aspects of his work are unsatisfactory
   B. *undesirable*; once the evaluation has been submitted, there is no point in reconsidering it
   C. *desirable*; once the evaluation has been submitted, there is no point in reconsidering it but a discussion of the employee's weaknesses may help
   D. *undesirable*; it would have been better to explain how you arrived at your evaluation
   E. *desirable*; entering into a general argument is bad for the discipline of an organization

12. The chief of a central files bureau which has 50 employees customarily spends a considerable portion of his time in spot-checking the files, reviewing material being transferred from active to inactive files and similar activities. 12.____
From the viewpoint of the department top management, the MOST pertinent evaluation which can be made on the basis of this information is that the
   A. supervisor is conscientious and hardworking
   B. bureau may need additional staff
   C. supervisor has not made a sufficient delegation of authority and responsibility
   D. bureau needs an in-service training course as the work of its employees requires an abnormal amount of review
   E filing system employed may be inadequate

13. Assume that you are in charge of a unit with 40 employees. The department head requests immediate preparation of a special and rather complicated report which will take about a day to complete if everyone in your unit works on it. 13.____
After breaking the job into simple components and assigning each component to an employee, should more than one person be instructed on the procedure to be followed on each component?
   A. *No*; the procedure would be a waste of time in this instance
   B. *Yes*; it is always desirable to have a replacement available in the event of illness or any other emergency
   C. *No*; in general, as long as an employee's job performance is satisfactory, there is no need to train an alternate
   D. *Yes*; the presence of more than one person in a unit who can perform a given task tends to prevent the formation of a bottleneck
   E. *No*; there is, in general, no need to train more than one employee in the performance of a special job

14. A new employee who has shown that she is capable of performing superior work during the first month of her employment falls far below this standard after the first month. 14.____
For the supervisor to wait until the end of the probationary period and then recommend that she be discharged if her work is still unsatisfactory is
   A. *undesirable*; she should have been discharged when her work became unsatisfactory
   B. *desirable*; there is no place in the civil service for unsatisfactory employees
   C. *undesirable*; he should immediately attempt to determine the cause of the poor performance
   D. *desirable*; the employee is entitled to an opportunity to prove herself
   E. *undesirable*; the employee is obviously capable of performing good work and simply requires some guidance from the supervisor

15. In order to make sure that work is completed on time, the unit supervisor should 15.____
    A. use the linear method of delegating responsibility
    B. pitch in and do as much of the work himself as he can
    C. schedule the work and keep himself informed of its progress
    D. not assign more than one person to any one task
    E. know the capabilities of his subordinates

16. One of the more effective ways to obtain optimum performance from employees is to keep them off balance by not letting them feel secure in the job; to permit an employee to feel secure is to invite him to settle into a comfortable rut. 16.____
    The point of view expressed in this statement is
    A. *correct*; studies have shown that the degree of effort put forth on a job generally varies directly with the degree of job insecurity
    B. *incorrect*; studies have shown that a relatively high degree of security is conducive to best job performance
    C. *correct*; while studies have shown that there is little relationship between security and job performance, what tendencies are present to support the point of view expressed
    D. *incorrect*; studies have shown that there is little relationship between security and job performance and what tendencies are present are opposed to the point of view expressed
    E. *correct*; while no specific studies have been made in this field, analogous studies made in similar fields show that permitting a feeling of security to develop results in decreased job performance

Questions 17-19.

DIRECTIONS: Questions 17 through 19 are to be answered on the basis of the following paragraph.

The supervisor of a large clerical and statistical division has assigned to one of the units under his supervision the preparation of a special statistical report required by the department head. The unit accepted the assignment without comment but soon ran into considerable difficulty because no one in his unit had had any statistical training.

17. If a result of this lack of training is that the report is not completed on time, although everyone has done all that could be expected, the responsibility for the failure rests with 17.____
    A. the department head
    B. the supervisor
    C. the unit head
    D. the employees in the unit
    E. no one

18. This incident indicates that the supervisory staff has insufficient knowledge of employee 18.____
    A. capabilities
    B. reaction to increased demands
    C. on-the-job training needs
    D. work habits
    E. ability to perform ordinary assignments

19. After working on the report for two days, the unit head notifies the supervisor that he will not be able to get the report out in the required time. He states that his staff will be completely trained in another day or two and that after preparing the report will be a simple matter. At this stage, the supervisor decides to have the statistical unit prepare the report. 19.____
This action on the part of the supervisor is
   A. *undesirable*; the unit head should be given an incentive to continue with his training program which may produce good results
   B. *desirable*; it is the most effective way in which the supervisor can show his displeasure with the unit head's failure
   C. *undesirable*; it may adversely affect the morale of the unit
   D. *desirable*; it will generally result in a better report completed in a shorter time
   E. *undesirable*; the time spent training the unit will be completely wasted

20. A supervisor criticizes a subordinate's work by telling him that he is disappointed with it. The supervisor states that the work is completely unsatisfactory, shows where it is bad, and says that improvement is expected. 20.____
This approach is usually
   A. *good*; the employee knows just where he stands
   B. *poor*; some favorable comment should be made at the same time if possible
   C. *good*; it is good policy to keep this type of interview as short as possible
   D. *poor*; the employee should be asked to explain why his work is poor
   E. *good*; the supervisor did not criticize the subordinate in front of other employees

Questions 21-25.

DIRECTIONS: Column I below lists five kinds of statistical data which are to be transformed into a chart or a graph for incorporation into the department annual report. Column II lists nine different kinds of graphs or charts. For each type of information listed in Column I, select the chart or graph from Column II by means of which it should be demonstrated.

COLUMN I | COLUMN II

21. The relationship between employees' occupational classification and their salaries, for all employees by occupational classification, showing minimum, maximum, and average salary in each group. 21.____

22. A comparison of the number of employees in the department, the departmental budget the number of employees in the operating divisions and the operating division budget for each year over a ten-year period. 22.____

A. 

B. 

C. 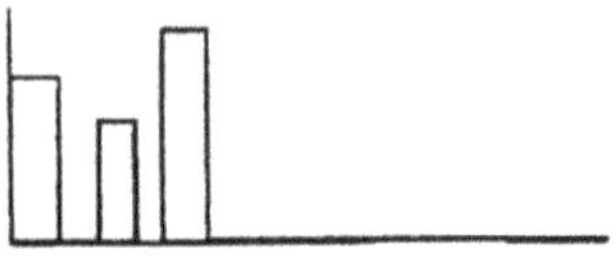

COLUMN I

23. The amount of money spent for each of the department's 10 most important functions during the past year. 23.____

24. The percentage of the department's budget spent for each of the department's activities for each year over a ten-year period. 24.____

25. The number of each kind of employee employed in the department over a period of twenty years and the total number of employees in the department for each of these periods. 25.____

COLUMN II

D. 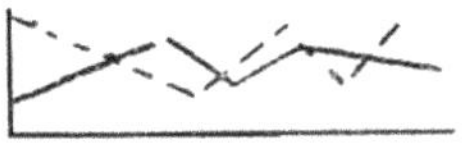

E. 

F. 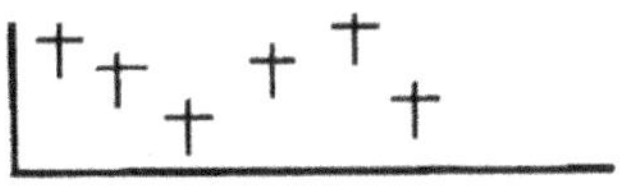

G. 

H. 

I. 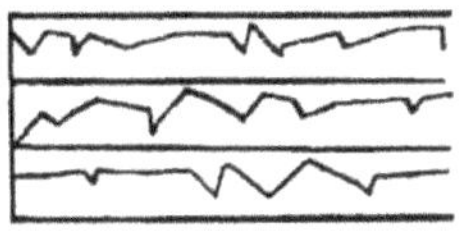

KEY (CORRECT ANSWERS)

1. B
2. D
3. A
4. C
5. B

6. B
7. E
8. C
9. A
10. E

11. D
12. C
13. A
14. C
15. C

16. B
17. B
18. A
19. D
20. B

21. F
22. D
23. C
24. H
25. G

TEST 2

DIRECTIONS: Each question or incomplete statement is followed by several suggested answers or completions. Select the one that BEST answers the question or completes the statement. *PRINT THE LETTER OF THE CORRECT ANSWER IN THE SPACE AT THE RIGHT.*

1. The report of the head of Unit Y to his bureau chief on the performance of a new clerical employee indicates that the performance is not up to the expected standard. After reading the report, the bureau chief transferred the employee to Unit X. 1.____
This action on the part of the bureau chief was
   A. in line with good personal practice; an employee who does poorly in one place may do better in another
   B. premature; an attempt to discover the cause of the poor performance should be made first
   C. desirable; personnel reports become meaningless unless acted upon at once
   D. undesirable; unsatisfactory employees should be dismissed and not transferred from unit to unit
   E. in the best interest of the organization; whenever a supervisor cannot get along with a subordinate for whatever reason, it is desirable to transfer the subordinate

2. Suppose that you have been consulted by a department head who wishes to initiate an in-service training course in his department. The department head suggests that, as a first step, a training course be initiated for supervisors in the department. 2.____
This suggestion is BEST characterized as
   A. *undesirable*; the supervisors are generally the persons least in need of work incentives
   B. *desirable*; it is generally cheaper and more effective to train a few supervisors than a large number of employees
   C. *undesirable*; supervisors may be held up to ridicule if they are isolated for training
   D. *desirable*; trained supervisors are needed to train employees
   E. *undesirable*; employees should be trained before supervisors

3. Any person thoroughly familiar with the specific steps in a particular class of work is well qualified to serve as a training course instructor in that work. 3.____
This statement is erroneous CHIEFLY because
   A. it is practically impossible for any instructor to be acquainted with all the specific steps sin a particular class of work
   B. what is true of one class of work is not necessarily true of other types of work
   C. a qualified instructor cannot be expected to have detailed information about many specific fields

D. the steps in any type of work are usually interrelated and not independent or unique
E. the quantity of information possessed by an instructor does not bear a direct relationship to the quality of instruction

4. Of the following, the MOST significant argument against making it compulsory for civil service employees to attend a training course is that 4.____
A. unwilling trainees will be penalized in any event by non-promotion
B. most training requires additional time and expense on the part of the trainee
C. training is highly desirable but not absolutely essential for adequate job performance
D. incompetent work is generally reflected in poor service ratings
E. trainees must be receptive if training is to be successful

5. There are four basic systems of job evaluation which have been extensively used by government and industry. 5.____
The one of the following which is NOT one of these is the _____ system.
A. Benchmark
B. Factor Comparison
C. Point
D. Job Classification
E. Ranking

6. Of the following, the CHIEF advantage derived by filling all vacancies in an organization by promotion from below rather than from outside the organization is that such a procedure 6.____
A. fills existing vacancies from the widest possible recruitment base
B. stimulates individual employees to improve their work habits
C. avoids personality difficulties likely to arise when an employee is assigned to supervise former colleagues
D. indirectly coordinates the work of different units by interchange of personnel
E. encourages reorientation and review of administrative procedures

7. Of the following, the CHIEF justification for a periodic classification audit is that 7.____
A. salaries should be readjusted at frequent intervals
B. some degree of personnel turnover should always be expected
C. a career service requires regular promotion opportunities
D. employees require frequent stimulation and encouragement
E. positions frequently change over a period of time

8. A classification analyst sorts jobs horizontally and vertically. 8.____
Of the following, the LEAST important job factor to be considered with respect to vertical placement is
A. independence of action and decision
B. consequence of errors
C. kind and character of work performed
D. degree of supervision received
E. determination of policy

9. Assume that you have been assigned to prepare a plan for conducting a large scale job classification survey. 9.____
Of the following, the BEST suggestion for reducing the number of appeals from the final allocations likely to be received after the classification study has been completed is to
   A. have supervisors check statements of employees on classification questionnaires
   B. allocate present positions to proposed classes according to jurisdictional assignments
   C. adjust salary to present level of work performed by employees
   D. allow employee participation throughout the classification process
   E. postpone controversial problems until simpler problems have been solved and a general blueprint laid down

10. A comment made by an employee about a training course was, *Oh, I suppose it's important for the job but it's a waste of time for me just to sit in that course and yawn while the instructor rambles on."* 10.____
The fundamental error in training methodology to which this criticism points is failure to provide
   A. goals for the students
   B. for individual differences
   C. connecting links between new and old material
   D. for student participation
   E. motivation for the subject matter of the course

11. You are preparing a long report addressed to your superior on a study which you have conducted for him. 11.____
The one of the following sections which should come FIRST in the report is a
   A. description of the working procedure utilized in the study
   B. description of the situation which exists
   C. summary of the conclusions of the survey
   D. discussion of possible objections to the report and their refutation
   E. description of the method of installing the recommendations

12. While setting up a reporting system to help the department planning section, an administrator proposed the policy that no overlap or duplication be permitted even if it meant that some minor areas were left uncovered. 12.____
This policy is
   A. *undesirable*; overlap is frequently necessary
   B. *desirable*; the presence of overlap and duplication indicates defective planning
   C. *undesirable*; setting up general policy in advance of the specific reporting system may lead to inflexibility
   D. *desirable*; it is not necessary to get complete coverage in order to be able to plan operations
   E. *undesirable*; duplication is preferable to leaving any area uncovered

Questions 13-15.

DIRECTIONS: Questions 13 through 15 are to be answered on the basis of the following paragraph.

Prior to revising its child care program, a department feels that it is necessary to get some information from the mothers served by the existing program in order to determine where changes are required. A questionnaire is to be constructed to obtain this information.

13. Of the following points which can be taken into consideration in the construction of the questionnaire, the one which is of LEAST importance is 13.____
    A. that the data are to be put into punch cards
    B. the aspects of the program which seem to be in need of change
    C. the type of person who will fill out the questionnaire
    D. testing the questionnaire for ambiguity in advance of general distribution
    E. setting up a control group so that answers received can be compared to a standard

14. To discuss this questionnaire with all mothers who have been asked to answer it, before they actually fill it out, is 14.____
    A. *desirable*; the mothers may be able to offer valuable suggestions for changes in the form of the questionnaire
    B. *undesirable*; it is of some value but consumes too much valuable time
    C. *desirable*; cooperation and uniform interpretation will tend to be achieved
    D. *undesirable*; it may cause the answers to be biased
    E. *desirable*; the group will tend to support the program

15. Of the following items included in the questionnaire, the one which will be of LEAST assistance for comparing attitudes toward the program among different kinds of persons is 15.____
    A. name
    B. address
    C. age
    D. place of birth
    E. education

16. You have been asked, to prepare for public distribution, a statement dealing with a controversial matter. 16.____
    Of the following approaches, the one which would usually be MOST effective is to present your department's point of view
    A. as tersely as possible with no reference to any other matters
    B. developed from ideas and facts well known to most readers
    C. and show all the statistical data and techniques which were used in arriving at it
    D. in such a way that the controversial parts are omitted
    E. substantiated by supporting quotations from persons in the specialized field even if they are not well known

17. During a conference of administrative staff personnel, the department head discussing the letter prepared for his signature stated, *"Use no more words than are necessary to express your meaning."* 17.____
Following this rule in letter writing is, in general,
   A. *desirable*; considerable time will be saved in the preparation of correspondence
   B. *undesirable*; it is frequently necessary to elaborate on an explanation in order to make certain that the reader will understand
   C. *desirable*; terse statements give government letters a business-like air which impresses readers favorably
   D. *undesirable*; terse statements are generally cold and formal and produce an unfavorable reaction in the reader
   E. *desirable*; the use of more words than are necessary is likely to obscure the meaning and tire the reader

18. While you are designing the layout for a departmental procedure manual, it is suggested that you carefully arrange your reading material so that there will be a minimum amount of blank space on the page. 18.____
Of the following judgments of this suggestion, the one which is the MOST valid basis for action is that it is
   A. *bad*; readability and ease of reference will be decreased
   B. *good*; the cost of production can be decreased considerably without any great disadvantage
   C. *of little or no importance*; more or less blank space on the page will not affect the value of the manual
   D. *good*; it will make for a smaller, easier to handle book
   E. *bad*; replacement of outdated pages is made more difficult by having more material on a page

19. After the planning of an employee's procedure manual had been completed, the suggestion was made that the manual should be prepared and arranged so that changes could be made readily. 19.____
Of the following decisions with respect to this suggestion, the one which is MOST desirable from the viewpoint of good administration is that the suggestions should
   A. not be considered as it is generally impossible to prepare a satisfactory manual which will take everything into consideration
   B. be followed only if it does not conflict with the planned layout
   C. be used even if it is somewhat more costly than the planned layout
   D. be noted and acted upon at the next revision of the manual
   E. not be considered as this type of manual is more difficult to maintain properly

20. Assume that you are in charge of preparing a procedure manual of about 100 pages for a large clerical unit. After you have decided to use a looseleaf format, one of your subordinates proposes that only one side of the page be printed. 20.____

This proposal is
- A. *good*; replacement of obsolete pages is made easier
- B. *poor*; cost is increased
- C. *good*; provision is automatically made for employee's notes
- D. *poor*; it will increase the size of the manual, making it more difficult to use
- E *good*; indexing will be made easier

21. It may be assumed that if all departments had qualified personnel officers, not all departments would be lacking adequate training programs. However, the most cursory examination of the situation will show that some departments do not have adequate training programs. Thus, we must conclude that some of them lack qualified personnel officers. 21.____
The argument presented in the report is
    - A. *correct*; the conclusion follows logically from the assumption and the facts
    - B. *not correct*; what can be concluded is that no department has a qualified personnel officer
    - C. *not correct*; no conclusion with respect to the presence of personnel officers in departments can be drawn from the information
    - D. *not correct*; what can be concluded is that the absence of an adequate training program in a department implies the absence of a personnel officer
    - E. *correct*; but the conclusion is false as the hypothesis is not true

22. In a study of the relationship between a fixed discipline policy and the incidence of lateness, it would be MOST informative to have data proving the statement: 22.____
    - A. In those organizations in which there are no fixed discipline policy, the incidence of lateness is variable.
    - B. The incidence of lateness has not decreased in those organizations where fixed discipline policies have been abandoned.
    - C. The incidence of lateness and the discipline policy vary from organization to organization.
    - D. Discipline policies sometimes ignore the problem of lateness.
    - E. In organizations with a fixed discipline policy, the incidence of lateness is variable.

23. The data prove that an increase in the number of clerks performing filing work results in an increased cost per item filed. 23.____
On the basis of these data, we can be certain that
    - A. if filing costs per item filed increase, it is caused by an increase in the number of clerks filing
    - B. if filing costs per item filed decrease, the number of clerks filing cannot be increasing
    - C. if the number of clerks filing is changed, the unit cost per filing will change
    - D. if the number of clerks filing is not increased, the cost per unit filed will not increase
    - E. if the number of clerks filing is decreased, the cost per item filed will decrease

24. Each unit either has sufficient space assigned to it or it has not. No unit which has insufficient space assigned to it has neglected to ask for additional space. From these data, we can state 24.____
   A. units with sufficient space have not asked for additional space
   B. only units which have sufficient space have not asked for additional space
   C. nothing about the relationship between the need for additional space and requests made for additional space
   D. all units which have requested additional space have insufficient space
   E. no units which have requested additional space have sufficient space

25. One argument which is presented against a strict career system in the civil service is as follows: 25.____
   The employees who are recruited today for low-level jobs become the administrators of tomorrow. At the present time the employees we are attracting for the low-level jobs are untrained and poorly educated. Thus, it follows that the administrators of tomorrow will be untrained and poorly educated.
   The one of the following which is a CORRECT criticism of the reasoning is that
   A. the argument is logically correct but the conclusion is false as the hypothesis that we are attracting untrained and poorly educated people for our low-level job is false
   B. the conclusion does not follow logically from hypotheses
   C. the argument is logically correct, but the conclusion is false because it is a false hypothesis that tomorrow's administrators will come from employees who hold low-level jobs
   D. the argument is logically correct and the conclusion is correct
   E. while the argument is logically correct and the hypotheses are not demonstrably false, the argument ignores the realities of the case that those who are untrained today may be trained tomorrow

KEY (CORRECT ANSWERS)

1.	B	11.	C
2.	D	12.	E
3.	E	13.	E
4.	E	14.	C
5.	A	15.	A
6.	B	16.	B
7.	E	17.	E
8.	C	18.	A
9.	D	19.	C
10.	D	20.	A

21.	C
22.	B
23.	B
24.	B
25.	B

TEST 3

DIRECTIONS: Each question or incomplete statement is followed by several suggested answers or completions. Select the one that BEST answers the question or completes the statement. *PRINT THE LETTER OF THE CORRECT ANSWER IN THE SPACE AT THE RIGHT.*

1. Surveying modern administration, it becomes clear that there is GREATEST need at present for administrators with 1.____
   A. a good knowledge of personnel administration
   B. the ability to write good reports
   C. a working knowledge of modern methods analysis
   D. a broad rather than specialized viewpoint
   E. the ability to analyze complicated fiscal programs

2. The one of the following which is a fundamental obstacle to effective planning in MOST governmental agencies is 2.___
   A. inadequate staff or resources
   B. the absence of the properly centralized administration
   C. the absence of clearly defined objective and constituent programs
   D. the neglect of analysis of ways and means
   E. the absence of functional boundaries for units and individuals

3. A department consists of several independent bureaus, each responsible to the commissioner for its own planning, operation, and reporting, a central personnel unit and the commissioner's office consisting of a secretary and several clerks to handle public relations. 3.____
   The one of the following *undesirable* characteristics which is MOST likely to arise in this organization is
   A. absence of planning
   B. weak and ineffectual leadership
   C. failure to have employees properly trained
   D. a lack of an easily understandable goal
   E. duplication of work

4. The one of the following practices which is MOST likely to lead to confusion, recrimination and jurisdictional conflict among the bureaus of a department is the failure to 4.____
   A. make clear and unambiguous assignments
   B. systematically subdivide the work
   C. explain general policy to those responsible for its achievement
   D. allocate equitably available resources
   E. set up uniform operating procedures for all units

5. The one of the following which is MOST likely to occur in an over-specialized administrative set-up is 5.____
   A. inability to recruit proper personnel to fill over-specialized positions
   B. improper supervision
   C. failure of employees to realize the broad implications of their work

D. lack of proper decentralization of authority, as emphasis on specialization goes hand-in-hand with over-centralization
E. inability to solve technical problems which are not entirely in one specialty

6. Of the following, the LEAST valid reason for a department head continuing to require that a weekly report be forwarded to him, is that the report forms a basis for 6.____
   A. measuring performance
   B. making decisions
   C. revising policy
   D. the execution of the mission of the unit which receives it
   E. the operation of the unit which is required to prepare it

7. Administrators must learn not to farm out essential functions to unintegrated agencies, but to organize all responsibilities in unified but decentralized hierarchies. 7.____
   A problem which an administrator may be expected to face if he has not learned this is that
   A. the organization fails to develop administrators capable of independent action
   B. issues will not be posed at the level where decisions should be made
   C. relationships with the public will not be satisfactory
   D. it will be difficult to achieve administrative control or get agreement on departmental action
   E. individual agencies will be unable to complete the work scheduled

8. The central staff planning unit within any organization includes in its functions helping to plan policy at one extreme and planning detailed execution at the other extreme. 8.____
   With respect to the actual execution, the planning activity should
   A. have no concern with it
   B. simply forward and explain new plans
   C. have only the responsibility of explaining in the form of plans the objectives of top management
   D. keep track of how the plans are working out but make no attempt to supervise their execution
   E. supervise the execution of new plans

9. The head of a department assigned final responsibility for the training function to the personnel office. 9.____
   This assignment was
   A. *undesirable*; this type of centralization prevents a staff organization from carrying out staff functions
   B. *desirable*; experience has shown that centralization of this type results in more efficient and economic operation
   C. *undesirable*; the personnel office usually does not have the technical "know how" to carry this responsibility
   D. *desirable*; if training is left to the line officials, it never is accomplished
   E. *undesirable*; this responsibility must rest with the supervisor

10. A department head insisted that operating officials participate in the development of new procedures along with the planning section. 10.____
Participation of this type is, on the whole,
   A. *desirable*; operating realities are more likely to be considered
   B. *undesirable*; the inclusion of conflicting views before the plan is drawn may result in no plan
   C. *desirable*; plans will be more flexible and objectives more clearly defined
   D. *undesirable*; the operating officials should decide to what extent they wish to participate with no pressure from the top
   E. *desirable*; to back down on a procedure once it has been decided upon is a sign of weakness

11. Much of the current criticism of the administration of large organizations is basically a criticism of our failure to place the same emphasis on accountability that we do on authority and responsibility. 11.____
The one of the following acts which is MOST likely to insure accountability for the discharge of responsibilities inherent in the delegation of authority is the
   A. establishment of appropriate reports and controls
   B. organization of a methods analysis section
   C. delegation of authority so made as to support functional or homogeneous activities
   D. delegation of authority so made as to preserve unity of command
   E. decentralization of responsibility and authority

12. This statement has been made: 12.____
A man who is a top-notch executive in one organization would make a top-notch executive in any other organization, even if the organizations are as diverse as a sales agency and a research foundation.
This statement is, in general,
   A. *correct*; the characteristics required for a good executive are invariant with respect to organization
   B. *incorrect*; there is no way of predicting how a good executive in one organization would be in any other
   C. *correct*; while the characteristics required for a good executive vary from organization to organization, the common core requirements are great enough to insure similar performance
   D. *incorrect*; although some prediction can be made, different types of organizations require different types of executives
   E. *correct*; success as an executive does not depend upon "characteristics" but on the man; if he is able to direct and execute in one organization he will be able to do so in any other

13. Reported information is not needed at levels higher than those at which decisions are made on the basis of the information reported. 13.____
This statement is, in general,
   A. *correct*; if no action is to be taken on the basis of the information, the information is unnecessary
   B. *incorrect*; all information is of importance in arriving at a sound decision

C. *correct*; levels below the one at which the decision is made have need of the information
D. *incorrect*; levels below the one at which the decision is made do not have need of the information
E. *correct*; decisions should be made on the basis of information reported

14. Of the following, the characteristic of an organization which BEST shows that the organizational hierarchy is effective is that 14.____
A. the department head commands the respect of the employees
B. the organization is sufficiently flexible to assume functions in fields not related to his major field of endeavor
C. responsibility has been appropriately delegated throughout the organization
D. the department continues to function effectively even though there is continual turnover in the higher supervisory ranks
E. no employee in the organization is subject to orders from more than one source

15. It is only because the primary purpose of traditional discipline has been to preserve the structure of command that a need has arisen for ameliorative safeguards such as a formal statement of "cause," right of hearing, and right of appeal. 15.____
The BEST current practice with respect to discipline is that
A. few ameliorative safeguards of the kind enumerated are desirable as their presence hurts the public service
B. discipline is a means of controlling deviations from established authority
C. the safeguards enumerated are not sufficient for the protection of the employee
D. discipline should be based upon education, persuasion, and consultation
E. unquestioned obedience to each order should not be expected but that a supervisor should be prepared at all times to demonstrate the reasonableness of his requests

16. Of the following types of work, the one for which a manual process is MOST usually to be preferred over a mechanized process is one in which the transactions are very 16.____
A. numerous B. similar C. dissimilar
D. predictable E. unpredictable

17. Work flow charts are used in an organization PRIMARILY because they 17.____
A. indicate present and future objectives clearly
B. are frequently used records
C. clearly indicate when each operation will be performed
D. summarize the work procedures of the organization
E. tend to clarify thinking by presenting certain facts clearly

18. With respect to a report prepared by an IBM installation, the one of the following changes which is LEAST likely to cause a change in the procedure for preparing the report is a change in the 18.____
   A. volume of work
   B. source documents
   C. final report
   D. employees assigned
   E. time allowed for the preparation of the report

19. The one of the following which is NOT necessarily a characteristic of a good buying procedure is that it 19.____
   A. provides for proper analysis of purchases made
   B. is simple
   C. makes provision for substitutions where possible and necessary
   D. makes sealed bids mandatory
   E. recruits many bidders

20. Data relating to the operation of any unit should be accumulated and periodically summarized and analyzed PRIMARILY in order to 20.____
   A. point out the most efficient and least efficient workers
   B. determine the relative value of each procedure
   C. locate the elements of an operation which are unusually efficient or inefficient
   D. evaluate the importance of maintaining operating records and quotas
   E. compare the work performed by comparable units

21. Of the following, the MAJOR function of an administrative planning and research staff units is to 21.____
   A. investigate trouble points in the organization
   B. reorganize inefficient units
   C. assist the executive to plan future operations
   D. conduct continuous investigations and planning
   E. write the necessary operation and procedure manuals

22. The one of the following which does NOT require definition when setting up a work measurement system is the 22.____
   A. level of work accomplishment at which to measure
   B. work unit in which to measure
   C. time unit by which to measure
   D. acceptable quota for each activity
   E. reporting system to be used

23. During a discussion of the time unit that would be appropriate to measure employee-time in a work measurement program in a public agency, the man-day was suggested. 23.____
   This unit is
   A. *satisfactory*; record keeping will be kept to a minimum
   B. *unsatisfactory*; it will be difficult to verify the unit against official time records

C. *satisfactory*; it will be easy to verify the unit against official time records
D. *unsatisfactory*; its use will unnecessarily complicate record keeping
E. *satisfactory*; it permits more meaningful comparisons to be made between equal periods of time

24. As part of a space layout survey, an administrator instructed his subordinates to study the flow of work and sequence of operating procedures. 24.____
His MAJOR purposes in doing this was to determine
A. the physical distribution and movement of personnel, material, and equipment
B. the amount of space which is available and the amount of space which will be required
C. the order in which the component steps in the different procedures are performed
D. what future requirements will be, based on observable present trend
E. how the distribution of personnel to various organization units is related to their space requirements

25. Before discussing a proposed office layout, the administrative officer stated, *"We intend to have a minimum number of private offices. We will assign private offices only where quiet is deemed essential or confidential conferences are required."* 25.____
The one of the following which is usually the MOST valid reason for this rule is that it
A. permits proper placing of employees who deal with the public
B. makes it easier to locate supervisors near the units they control
C. tends to ensure that the work of each unit will flow continually forward within itself
D. allows placing complementary units close together
E. makes clerical supervision easier

KEY (CORRECT ANSWERS)

1. D
2. C
3. E
4. A
5. C

6. E
7. D
8. D
9. E
10. A

11. A
12. D
13. A
14. C
15. D

16. C
17. E
18. D
19. D
20. C

21. D
22. D
23. D
24. A
25. E

EXAMINATION SECTION

TEST 1

DIRECTIONS: Each question or incomplete statement is followed by several suggested answers or completions. Select the one that BEST answers the question or completes the statement. *PRINT THE LETTER OF THE CORRECT ANSWER IN THE SPACE AT THE RIGHT.*

1. In almost every organization there is a nucleus of highly important functions commonly designated as *management*. 1.____
   Which of the following statements BEST characterizes *management*?
   A. Getting things done through others
   B. The highest level of intelligence in any organization
   C. The process whereby democratic and participative activities are maximized
   D. The *first among equals*

2. Strategies in problem-solving are important to anyone aspiring to advancement in the field of administration. 2.____
   Which of the following is BEST classified as the first step in the process of problem-solving?
   A. Collection and organization of data
   B. The formulation of a plan
   C. The definition of the problem
   D. The development of a method and methodology

3. One of the objectives of preparing a budget is to
   A. create optimistic goals which each department can attempt to meet
   B. create an overall company goals by combining the budgets of the various departments
   C. be able to compare planned expenditures against actual expenditures
   D. be able to identify accounting errors

4. The rise in demand for *systems* personnel in industrial and governmental organizations over the past five years has been extraordinary. 4.____
   In which of the following areas would a *systems* specialist assigned to an agency be LEAST likely to be of assistance?
   A. Developing, recommending, and establishing an effective cost and inventory system
   B. Development and maintenance of training manuals
   C. Reviewing existing work procedures and recommending improvements
   D. Development of aptitude tests for new employees

5. Management experts have come to the conclusion that the traditional forms of motivation used in industry and government, which emphasize authority over and economic rewards for the employee, are no longer appropriate. 5.____

To which of the following factors do such experts attribute the GREATEST importance in producing this change?

A. The desire of employees to satisfy material needs has become greater and more complex.
B. The desire for social satisfaction has become the most important aspect of the job for the average worker.
C. With greater standardization of work processes, there has been an increase in the willingness of workers to accept discipline.
D. In general, employee organizations have made it more difficult for management to fire an employee.

6. In preparing a budget, it is usually considered advisable to start the initial phases of preparation at the operational level of management. 6.____
Of the following, the justification that management experts usually advance as MOST reasonable for this practice is that operating managers, as a consequence of their involvement, will

A. develop a background in finance or accounting
B. have an understanding of the organizational structure
C. tend to feel responsible for carrying out budget activities
D. have the ability to see the overall financial picture

7. An administrative officer has been asked by his superior to write a concise, factual report with objective conclusions and recommendations based on facts assembled by other researchers. 7.____
Of the following factors, the administrative officer should give LEAST consideration to

A. the educational level of the person or persons for whom the report is being prepared
B. the use to be made of the report
C. the complexity of the problem
D. his own feelings about the importance of the problem

8. In an agency, upon which of the following is a supervisor's effectiveness MOST likely to depend? 8.____
The

A. degree to which a supervisor allows subordinates to participate in the decision-making process and the setting of objectives
B. degree to which a supervisor's style meets management's objectives and subordinates' needs
C. strength and forcefulness of the supervisor in pursuing his objectives
D. expertise and knowledge of the supervisor has about the specific work to be done

9. For authority to be effective, which of the following is the MOST basic requirement? 9.____
Authority must be

A. absolute B. formalized C. accepted D. delegated

10. Management no longer abhors the idea of employees taking daily work breaks, but prefers to schedule such breaks rather than to allot to each employee a standard amount of free time to be taken off during the day as he wishes. 10.____
Which of the following BEST expresses the reason management theorists give for the practice of scheduling such breaks?
   A. Many jobs fall into natural work units which are scheduled, and the natural time to take a break is at the end of the unit
   B. Taking a scheduled break permits socialization and a feeling of accomplishment
   C. Managers have concluded that scheduling rest periods seems to reduce the incidence of unscheduled ones
   D. Many office workers who really need such breaks are hesitant about taking them unless they are scheduled

11. The computer represents one of the major developments of modern technology. It is widely used in both scientific and managerial activities because of its many advantages. 11.____
Which of the following is NOT an advantage gained by management in the use of the computer?
A computer
   A. provides the manager with a greatly enlarged memory so that he can easily be provided with data for decision making
   B. relieves the manager of basic decision-making responsibility, thereby giving him more time for directing and controlling
   C. performs routine, repetitive calculations with greater precision and reliability than employees
   D. provides a capacity for rapid simulations of alternative solutions to problem solving

12. A supervisor of a unit in a division is usually responsible for all of the following EXCEPT 12.____
   A. the conduct of subordinates in the achievement of division objectives
   B. maintaining quality standards in the unit
   C. the protection and care of materials and equipment in the unit
   D. performing the most detailed tasks in the unit himself

13. You have been assigned to teach a new employee the functions and procedures of your office. 13.____
In your introductory talk, which of the following approaches is PREFERABLE?
   A. Advise the new employee of the employee benefits and services available to him, over and above his salary
   B. Discuss honestly the negative aspects of departmental procedures and indicate methods available to overcome them
   C. Give the new employee an understanding of the general purpose of office procedures and functions and of their relevance to departmental objectives
   D. Give a basic and detailed explanation of the operations of your office, covering all functions and procedures

14. It is your responsibility to assign work to several clerks under your supervision. One of the clerks indignantly refuses to accept an assignment and asks to be given something else. He has not yet indicated why he does not want the assignment, but is sitting there glaring at you, awaiting your reaction. 14.____
Of the following, which is the FIRST action you should take?
   A. Ask the employee into your office in order to reprimand him and tell him emphatically that he must accept the assignment
   B. Talk to the employee privately in an effort to find the reason for his indignation and refusal, and then base your action upon your findings
   C. Let the matter drop for a day or two to allow the employee to cool off before you insist that he accept the assignment
   D. Inform the employee quietly and calmly that as his supervisor you have selected him for this assignment and that you fully expect him to accept it

15. Administrative officers are expected to be able to handle duties delegated to them by their supervisors and to be able, as they advance in status, to delegate tasks to assistants. 15.____
When considering whether to delegate tasks to a subordinate, which of the following questions should be LEAST important to an administrative officer?
In the delegated tasks,
   A. how significant are the decisions to be made, and how much consultation will be involved?
   B. to what extent is uniformity and close coordination of activity required?
   C. to what extent must speedy-on-the-spot decisions be made?
   D. to what extent will delegation relieve the administrative officer of his burden of responsibility?

16. A functional forms file is a collection of forms which are grouped by 16.____
   A. purpose B. department C. title D. subject

17. All of the following are reasons to consult a records retention schedule except one. 17.____
Which one is that?
To determine
   A. whether something should be filed
   B. how long something should stay in file
   C. who should be assigned to filing
   D. when something on file should be destroyed

18. Listed below are four of the steps in the process of preparing correspondence for filing. 18.____
If they were to be put in logical sequence, the SECOND step would be
   A. preparing cross-reference sheets or cards
   B. coding the correspondence using a classification system
   C. sorting the correspondence in the order to be filed
   D. checking for follow-up action required and preparing a follow-up slip

19. New material added to a file folder should USUALLY be inserted 19.____
    A. in the order of importance (the most important in front)
    B. in the order of importance (the most important in back)
    C. chronologically (most recent in front)
    D. chronologically (most recent in back)

20. An individual is looking for a name in the white pages of a telephone directory. Which of the following BEST describes the system of filing found there? 20.____
A(n) _____ file
    A. alphabetic B. sequential C. locator D. index

21. The MAIN purpose of a tickler file is to 21.____
    A. help prevent overlooking matters that require future attention
    B. check on adequacy of past performance
    C. pinpoint responsibility for recurring daily tasks
    D. reduce the volume of material kept in general files

22. Which of the following BEST describes the process of reconciling a bank statement? 22.____
    A. Analyzing the nature of the expenditures made by the office during the preceding month
    B. Comparing the statement of the bank with the banking records maintained in the office
    C. Determining the liquidity position by reading the bank statement carefully
    D. Checking the service charges noted on the bank statement

23. From the viewpoint of preserving agency or institutional funds, which of the following is the LEAST acceptable method for making a payment? 23.____
A check made out to
    A. cash B. a company
    C. an individual D. a partnership

24. In general, the CHIEF economy of using multicopy forms is in 24.____
    A. the paper on which the form is printed
    B. printing the form
    C. employee time
    D. carbon paper

25. Suppose your supervisor has asked you to develop a form to record certain information needed. 25.____
The FIRST thing you should do is to
    A. determine the type of data that will be recorded repeatedly so that it can be preprinted
    B. study the relationship of the form to the job to be accomplished so that the form can be planned
    C. determine the information that will be recorded in the same place on each copy of the form so that it can be used as a check
    D. find out who will be responsible for supplying the information so that space can be provided for their signatures

26. An administrative officer in charge of a small fund for buying office supplies has just written a check to Charles Laird, a supplier, and has sent the check by messenger to him. A half-hour later, the messenger telephones the administrative officer. He has lost the check. 26.____
Which of the following is the MOST important action for the administrative officer to take under these circumstances?
   A. Ask the messenger to return and write a report describing the loss of the check
   B. Make a note on the performance record of the messenger who lost the check
   C. Take the necessary steps to have payment stopped on the check
   D. Refrain from doing anything since the check may be found shortly

27. A petty cash fund is set up PRIMARILY to 27.____
   A. take care of small investments that must be made from time to time
   B. take care of small expenses that arise from time to time
   C. provide a fund to be used as the office wants to use it with little need to maintain records
   D. take care of expenses that develop during emergencies, such as machine breakdowns and fires

28. Of the following, which is usually the MOST important guideline in writing business letters? 28.____
A letter should be
   A. neat
   B. written in a formalized style
   C. written in clear language intelligible to the reader
   D. written in the past tense

29. Suppose you are asked to edit a policy statement. You note that personal pronouns like *you*, *we*, and *I* are used freely. 29.____
Which of the following statements BEST applies to this use of personal pronouns?
It
   A. is proper usage because written business language should not be different from carefully spoken business language
   B. requires correction because is it ungrammatical
   C. is proper because it is clearer and has a warmer tone
   D. requires correction because policies should be expressed in an impersonal manner

30. Good business letters are coherent. 30.____
To be coherent means to
   A. keep only one unifying idea in the message
   B. present the total message
   C. use simple, direct words for the message
   D. tie together the various ideas in the message

31. Proper division of a letter into paragraphs requires that the writer of business letters should, as much as possible, be sure that 31.____
   A. each paragraph is short
   B. each paragraph develops discussion of just one topic
   C. each paragraph repeats the theme of the total message
   D. there are at least two paragraphs for every message

32. An editor is given a letter with this initial paragraph: 32.____
We have received your letter, which we read with interest, and we are happy to respond to your question. In fact, we talked with several people in our office to get ideas to send to you.
Which of the following is MOST reasonable for the editor to conclude?
The paragraph is
   A. concise
   B. communicating something of value
   C. unnecessary
   D. coherent

33. As soon as you pick up the phone, a very angry caller begins immediately to complain about city agencies and *red tape*. He says that he has been shifted to two or three different offices. It turns out that he is seeking information which is not immediately available to you. You believe you know, however, where it can be found. 33.____
Which of the following actions is the BEST one for you to take?
   A. To eliminate all confusion, suggest that the caller write the mayor stating explicitly what he wants
   B. Apologize by telling the caller how busy city agencies now are, but also tell him directly that you do not have the information he needs
   C. Ask for the caller's telephone number and assure him you will call back after you have checked further
   D. Give the caller the name and telephone number of the person who might be able to help, but explain that you are not positive he will get results

34. Suppose that one of your duties is to dictate responses to routine requests from the public for information. A letter writer asks for information which, as expressed in a one-sentence, explicit agency rule, cannot be given out to the public. 34.____
Of the following ways of answering the letter, which is the MOST efficient?
   A. Quote verbatim that section of the agency rules which prohibit giving this information to the public
   B. Without quoting the rule, explain why you cannot accede to the request and suggest alternative sources
   C. Describe how carefully the request was considered before classifying it as subject to the rule forbidding the issuance of such information
   D. Acknowledge receipt of the letter and advise that the requested information is not released to the public

35. Suppose you assist in supervising a staff which has rather high morale, and your own supervisor asks you to poll the staff to find out who will be able to work overtime this particular evening to help complete emergency work. 35.____
Which of the following approaches would be MOST likely to win their cooperation while maintaining their morale?
   A. Tell them that the better assignments will be given only to those who work overtime
   B. Tell them that occasional overtime is a job requirement
   C. Assure them they'll be doing you a personal favor
   D. Let them know clearly why the overtime is needed

36. Suppose that you have been asked to write and to prepare for reproduction new departmental vacation leave regulations. 36.____
After you have written the new regulations, all of which fit on one page, which one of the following would be the BESST method of reproducing 1,000 copies?
   A. An outside private printer, because you can best maintain confidentiality using this technique
   B. Xeroxing, because the copies will have the best possible appearance
   C. Typing copies, because you will be certain that there are the fewest possible errors
   D. Including it in the next company newsletter

37. Administration is the center, but not necessarily the source, of all ideas for procedural improvement. 37.____
The MOST significant implication that this principle bears for the administrative officer is that
   A. before procedural improvements are introduced, they should be approved by a majority of the staff
   B. it is the unique function of the administrative officer to derive and introduce procedural improvements
   C. the administrative officer should derive ideas and suggestions for procedural improvement from all possible sources, introducing any that promise to be effective
   D. the administrative officer should view employee grievances as the chief source of procedural improvements

38. Your bureau is assigned an important task. 38.____
Of the following, the function that you, as an administrative officer, can LEAST reasonably be expected to perform under these circumstances is
   A. division of the large job into individual tasks
   B. establishment of *production lines* within the bureau
   C. performance personally of a substantial share of all the work
   D. check up to see that the work has been done well

39. Suppose that you have broken a complex job into its smaller components before making assignments to the employees under your jurisdiction. 39.____
Of the following, the LEAST advisable procedure to follow from that point is to
    A. give each employee a picture of the importance of his work for the success of the total job
    B. establish a definite line of work flow and responsibility
    C. post a written memorandum of the best method for performing each job
    D. teach a number of alternative methods for doing each job

40. As an administrative officer, you are requested to draw up an organization chart of the whole department. 40.____
Of the following, the MOST important characteristic of such a chart is that it will
    A. include all peculiarities and details of the organization which distinguish it from any other
    B. be a schematic representation of purely administrative functions within the department
    C. present a modification of the actual departmental organization in the light of principles of scientific management
    D. present an accurate picture of the lines of authority and responsibility

KEY (CORRECT ANSWERS)

1.	A	11.	B	21.	A	31.	B
2.	C	12.	D	22.	B	32.	C
3.	C	13.	C	23.	A	33.	C
4.	D	14.	B	24.	C	34.	A
5.	D	15.	D	25.	B	35.	D
6.	C	16.	A	26.	C	36.	B
7.	D	17.	C	27.	B	37.	C
8.	B	18.	A	28.	C	38.	C
9.	C	19.	C	29.	D	39.	D
10.	C	20.	A	30.	D	40.	D

TEST 2

DIRECTIONS: Each question or incomplete statement is followed by several suggested answers or completions. Select the one that BEST answers the question or completes the statement. *PRINT THE LETTER OF THE CORRECT ANSWER IN THE SPACE AT THE RIGHT.*

Questions 1-10.

DIRECTIONS: In each of Questions 1 through 10, a pair of related words written in capital letters is followed by four other pairs of words. For each question, select the pair of words which MOST closely expresses a relationship similar to that of the pair in capital letters.

SAMPLE QUESTION:
BOAT – DOCK

A. air plane – hangar
B. rain – snow
C. cloth – cotton
D. hunger - food

Choice A is the answer to this sample question since, of the choices given, the relationship between airplane and hangar is most similar to the relationship between boat and dock.

1. AUTOMOBILE – FACTORY 1.____
   A. tea – lemon
   B. wheel – engine
   C. pot – flower
   D. paper – mill

2. GIRDER – BRIDGE 2.____
   A. petal – flower
   B. street – sidewalk
   C. meat – vegetable
   D. sun – storm

3. RADIUS – CIRCLE 3.____
   A. brick – building
   B. tie – tracks
   C. spoke – wheel
   D. axle – tire

4. DISEASE – RESEARCH 4.____
   A. death – poverty
   B. speech – audience
   C. problem – conference
   D. invalid – justice

5. CONCLUSION – INTRODUCTION 5.____
   A. commencement – beginning
   B. housing – motor
   C. caboose – engine
   D. train – cabin

6. SOCIETY – LAW 6.____
   A. baseball – rules
   B. jury – law
   C. cell – prisoner
   D. sentence – jury

7. PLAN – ACCOMPLISHMENT 7.____
   A. deed – fact
   B. method – success
   C. graph – chart
   D. rules – manual

8. ORDER – GOVERNMENT 8.____
   A. chaos – administration
   B. confusion – pandemonium
   C. rule – stability
   D. despair – hope

9. TYRANNY – FREEDOM 9.____
   A. despot – mob
   B. wealth – poverty
   C. nobility – commoners
   D. dictatorship – democracy

10. FAX – LETTER 10.____
   A. hare – tortoise
   B. lie – truth
   C. number – word
   D. report – research

Questions 11-16.

DIRECTIONS: Questions 11 through 16 are to be answered SOLELY on the basis of the information given in the passage below.

Inherent in all organized endeavors is the need to resolve the individual differences involved in conflict. Conflict may be either a positive or negative factor, since it may lead to creativity, innovation, and progress, on the one hand, or it may result, on the other hand, in a deterioration or even destruction of the organization. Thus, some forms of conflict are desirable, whereas others are undesirable and ethically wrong.

There are three management strategies which deal with interpersonal conflict. In the "divide-and-rule strategy," management attempts to maintain control by limiting the conflict to those directly involved and preventing their disagreement from spreading to the larger group. The "suppression –of-differences strategy" entails ignoring conflicts or pretending they are irrelevant. In the "working-through-differences strategy," management actively attempts to solve or resolve intergroup or interpersonal conflicts. Of the three strategies, only the last directly attacks and has the potential for eliminating the causes of conflict. An essential part of this strategy, however, is its employment by a committed and relatively mature management team.

11. According to the above passage, the *divide-and-rule strategy* for dealing with conflict is the attempt to 11.____
   A. involve other people in the conflict
   B. restrict the conflict to those participating in it
   C. divide the conflict into positive and negative factors
   D. divide the conflict into a number of smaller ones

12. The word *conflict* is used in relation to both positive and negative factors in this passage. 12.____
Which one of the following words is MOST likely to describe the activity which the word *conflict*, in the sense of the passage, implies?
   A. Competition B. Cooperation C. Confusion D. Aggression

13. According to the above passage, which one of the following characteristics is shared by both the *suppression-of-difference strategy* and the *divide-and-rule strategy*? 13.____
    A. Pretending that conflicts are irrelevant
    B. Preventing conflicts from spreading to the group situation
    C. Failure to directly attack the causes of conflict
    D. Actively attempting to resolve interpersonal conflict

14. According to the above passage, the successful resolution of interpersonal conflict requires 14.____
    A. allowing the group to mediate conflicts between two individuals
    B. division of the conflict into positive and negative factors
    C. involvement of a committed, mature management team
    D. ignoring minor conflicts until they threaten the organization

15. Which can be MOST reasonably inferred from the above passage? 15.____
    A conflict between two individuals is LEAST likely to continue when management uses
    A. the *working-through-differences strategy*
    B. the *suppression-of-differences strategy*
    C. the *divide-and-rule strategy*
    D. a combination of all three strategies

16. According to the above passage, a DESIRABLE result of conflict in an organization is when conflict 16.____
    A. exposes production problems in the organization
    B. can be easily ignored by management
    C. results in advancement of more efficient managers
    D. leads to development of new methods

Questions 17-23.

DIRECTIONS: Questions 17 through 23 are to be answered SOLELY on the basis of the information given in the passage below.

Modern management places great emphasis on the concept of communication. The communication process consists of the steps through which an idea or concept passes from its inception by one person, the sender, until it is acted upon by another person, the receiver. Through an understanding of these steps and some of the possible barriers that may occur, more effective communication may be achieved. The first step in the communication process is ideation by the sender. This is the formation of the intended content of the message he wants to transmit. In the next step, encoding, the sender organizes his ideas into a series of symbols designed to communicate his message to his intended receiver. He selects suitable words or phrases that can be understood by the receiver, and he also selects the appropriate media to be used—for example, memorandum, conference, etc. The third step is transmission of the encoded message through selected channels in the organizational structure. In the fourth step, the receiver enters the process by tuning in to receive the message. If the receiver does not function, however, the message is lost. For example, if the message is oral, the receiver must be a good listener. The fifth step is decoding of the message by the receiver, as for example, by changing words into ideas. At this step, the decoded message may not be the same idea that the sender originally encoded because the sender and receiver have different perceptions regarding the meaning of certain words.

Finally, the receiver acts or responds. He may file the information, ask for more information, or take other action. There can be no assurance, however, that communication has taken place unless there is some type of feedback to the sender in the form of an acknowledgement that the message was received.

17. According to the above passage, *ideation* is the process by which the 17.____
    - A. sender develops the intended content of the message
    - B. sender organizes his ideas into a series of symbols
    - C. receiver tunes in to receive the message
    - D. receiver decodes the message

18. In the last sentence of the passage, the word *feedback* refers to the process by which the sender is assured that the 18.____
    - A. receiver filed the information
    - B. receiver's perception is the same as his own
    - C. message was received
    - D. message was poorly interpreted

19. Which one of the following BEST shows the order of the steps in the communication process as described in the passage? 19.____
    - A. 1 – ideation 2 – encoding
      3 – decoding 4 – transmission
      5 – receiving 6 – action
      7 – feedback to the sender
    - B. 1 – ideation 2 – encoding
      3 – transmission 4 – decoding
      5 – receiving 6 – action
      7 – feedback to the sender
    - C. 1 – ideation 2 – decoding
      3 – transmission 4 – receiving
      5 – encoding 6 – action
      7 – feedback to the sender
    - D. 1 – ideation 2 – encoding
      3 – transmission 4 – receiving
      5 – decoding 6 – action
      7 – feedback to the sender

20. Which one of the following BEST expresses the main theme of the passage? 20.____
    - A. Different individuals have the same perceptions regarding the meaning of words.
    - B. An understanding of the steps in the communication process may achieve better communication.
    - C. Receivers play a passive role in the communication process.
    - D. Senders should not communicate with receivers who transmit feedback.

21. The above passage implies that a receiver does NOT function properly when he 21.____
    A. transmits feedback
    B. files the information
    C. is a poor listener
    D. asks for more information

22. Which of the following, according to the above passage, is included in the SECOND step of the communication process? 22.____
    A. Selecting the appropriate media to be used in transmission
    B. Formulation of the intended content of the message
    C. Using appropriate media to respond to the receiver's feedback
    D. Transmitting the message through selected channels in the organization

23. The above passage implies that the *decoding* process is MOST NEARLY the reverse of the _____ process. 23.____
    A. transmission
    B. receiving
    C. feedback
    D. encoding

Questions 24-27.

DIRECTIONS: Questions 24 through 27 are to be answered SOLELY on the basis of the information given in the passage below.

A personnel researcher has at his disposal various approaches for obtaining information, analyzing it, and arriving at conclusions that have value in predicting and affecting the behavior of people at work. The type of method to be used depends on such factors as the nature of the research problem, the available data, and the attitude of those people being studied to the various kinds of approaches. While the experimental approach, with its use of control groups, is the most refined type of study, there are others that are often found useful in personnel research. Surveys, in which the researcher obtains facts on a problem from a variety of sources, are employed in research on wages, fringe benefits, and labor relations. Historical studies are used to trace the development of problems in order to understand them better and to isolate possible causative factors. Case studies are generally developed to explore all the details of a particular problem that is representative of other similar problems. A researcher chooses the most appropriate form of study for the problem he is investigating. He should recognize, however, that the experimental method, commonly referred to as the scientific method, if used validly and reliably, gives the most conclusive results.

24. The above statement discusses several approaches used to obtain information on particular problems. 24.____
    Which of the following may be MOST reasonably concluded from the passage?
    A(n)
    A. historical study cannot determine causative factors
    B. survey is often used in research on fringe benefits
    C. case study is usually used to explore a problem that is unique and unrelated to other problems
    D. experimental study is used when the scientific approach to a problem fails

25. According to the above passage, all of the following are factors that may determine the type of approach a researcher uses EXCEPT 25.____
    A. the attitudes of people toward being used in control groups
    B. the number of available sources
    C. his desire to isolate possible causative factors
    D. the degree of accuracy he requires

26. The words *scientific method*, used in the last sentence of the paragraph, refer to a type of study which, according to the paragraph, 26.____
    A. uses a variety of sources
    B. traces the development of problems
    C. uses control group
    D. analyzes the details of a representative problem

27. Which of the following can be MOST reasonably concluded from the above passage? 27.____
    In obtaining and analyzing information on a particular problem, a researcher employs the method which is the
    A. most accurate
    B. most suitable
    C. least expensive
    D. least time-consuming

Questions 28-31.

DIRECTIONS: Questions 28 through 31 are to be answered according to the information given in the following graph, which indicates at 5-year intervals the number of citations issued for various offenses from the year 2000 to the year 2020.

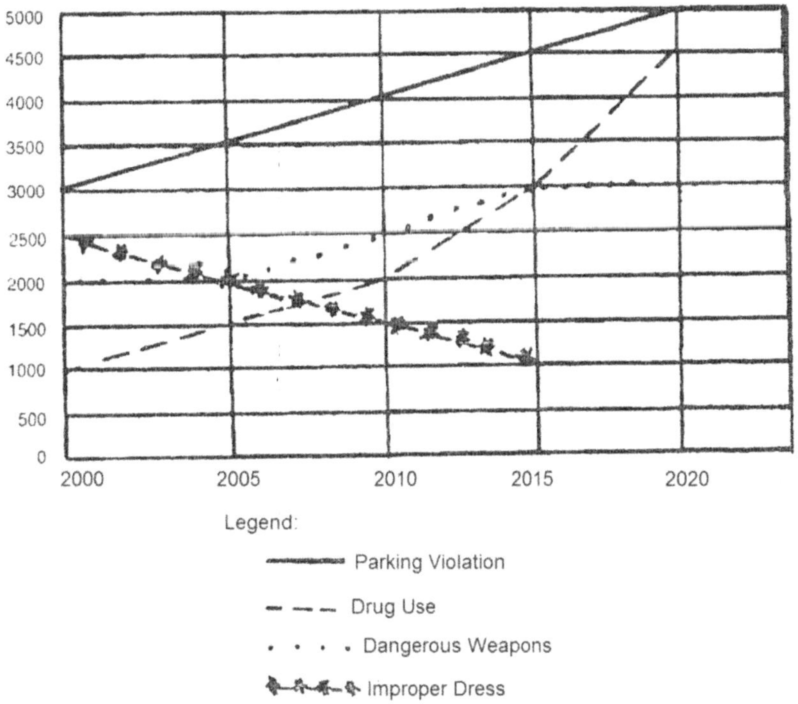

28. Over the 20-year period, which offense shows an AVERAGE rate of increase of more than 150 citations per year? 28.____
    A. Parking Violations B. Dangerous Weapons
    C. Drug Use D. None of the above

29. Over the 20-year period, which offense shows a CONSTANT rate of increase or decrease? 29.____
    A. Parking Violations B. Drug Use
    C. Dangerous Weapons D. Improper Dress

30. Which offense shows a TOTAL INCREASE OR DECREASE of 50% for the full 20-year period? 30.____
    A. Parking Violations B. Drug Use
    C. Dangerous Weapons D. Improper Dress

31. The percentage increase in total citations issued from 2005 to 2010 is MOST NEARLY 31.____
    A. 7% B. 11% C. 21% D. 41%

Questions 32-35.

DIRECTIONS: Questions 32 through 35 are to be answered SOLELY on the basis of the information given in the following chart, which shows the annual number of administrative actions completed for the four divisions of a bureau. Assume that the figures remain stable from year to year.

	DIVISIONS				
Administrative Actions	W	X	Y	Z	TOTALS
Telephone Inquiries Answered	8,000	6,800	7,500	4,800	27,100
Interviews Conducted	500	630	550	500	2,180
Applications Processed	15,000	18,000	14,500	9,500	57,000
Letters Typed	2,500	4,400	4,350	3,250	14,500
Reports Completed	200	250	100	50	600
Totals	26,200	30,080	27,000	18,100	101,380

32. In which division is the number of Applications Processed the GREATEST percentage of the total Administrative Action for that division? 32.____
    A. W B. X C. Y D. Z

33. The bureau chief is considering a plant that would consolidate the typing of letters in a separate unit. This unit would be responsible for the typing of letters for all divisions in which the number of letters typed exceeds 15% of the total number of Administrative Actions. 33.____
    Under this plan, which of the following divisions would CONTINUE to type its own letters?
    A. W and X B. W, X, and Y C. X and Y D. X and Z

34. The setting up of a central information service that would be capable of answering 25% of the whole bureau's telephone inquiries is under consideration. Under such a plan, the divisions would gain for other activities that time previously spent on telephone inquiries. 34.____
Approximately how much total time would such a service gain for all four divisions if it requires 5 minutes to answer the average telephone inquiry?
_____ hours.
A. 500 B. 515 C. 565 D. 585

35. Assume that the rate of production shown in the table can be projected as accurate for the coming year and that monthly output is constant for each type of administrative action within a division. Division Y is scheduled to work exclusively on a 4-month long special project during that year. During the period of the project, Division Y's regular workload will be divided evenly among the remaining divisions. 35.____
Using the figures in the table, what would be MOST NEARLY the percentage increase in the total Administrative Actions completed by Division Z for the year?
A. 8% B. 16% C. 25% D. 50%

36. You have conducted a traffic survey a 10 two-lane bridges and find the traffic between 4:30 and 5:30 P.M. average 665 cars per bridge that hour. You can't find the tabulation sheet for Bridge #7, but you know that 6066 cars were counted at the other 9 bridges. 36.____
Determine from this how many must have been counted at Bridge #7.
A. 584 B. 674 C. 665 D. 607

37. You pay temporary help $11.20 per hour and regular employees $12.00 per hour. Your workload is temporarily heavy, so you need 20 hours of extra regular employees' time to catch up. If you do this on overtime, you must pay time-and-a-half. If you use temporary help, it takes 25% more time to do the job. 37.____
What is the difference in cost between the two alternatives?
A. $20 more for temporary B. $40 more for temporary
C. $80 more for regular D. $136 more for regular

38. An experienced clerk can process the mailing of annual forms in 9 day. A new clerk takes 14 days to process them. 38.____
If they work together, how many days MOST NEARLY will it take to do the processing?
A. 4½ B. 5½ C. 6½ D. 7

39. A certain administrative aide is usually able to successfully handle 27% of all telephone inquiries without assistance. In a particular month, he receives 1,200 inquiries and handles 340 of them successfully on his own. 39.____
How many more inquiries has he handled successfully in that month than would have been expected of him based on his usual rate?
A. 10 B. 16 C. 24 D. 44

40. Suppose that on a scaled drawing of an office building floor, ½ inch represents three feet of actual floor dimensions. 40.____
A floor which is, in fact, 75 feet wide and 132 feet long has which of the following dimensions on this scaled drawing? _____ inches wide and _____ inches long.
A. 9.5; 20.5 B. 12.5; 22 C. 17;32 D. 25; 44

41. In a division of clerks and stenographers, 15 people are currently employed, 20% of whom are stenographers. 41.____
If management plans are to maintain the current number of stenographers, but to increase the clerical staff to the point where 12% of the total staff are stenographers, what is the MAXIMUM number of additional clerks that should be hired to meet these plans?
A. 3 B. 8 C. 10 D. 12

42. Suppose that a certain agency had a 2018 budget of $1,200,500. The 2019 budget was 7% higher than that of 2018, and the 2020 budget was 8% higher than that of 2019. 42.____
Of the following, which one is MOST NEARLY that agency's budget for 2020?
A. $1,177,624 B. $1,261,737 C. $1,265,575 D. $1,271,738

Questions 43-50.

DIRECTIONS: Your office keeps a file card record of the work assignments for all the employees in a certain bureau. On each card is the employee's name, a work assignment code number, and the date of this assignment. In this filing system, the employee's name is filed alphabetically, the work assignment code is filed numerically, and the date of assignment is filed chronologically (earliest date first).

Each of Questions 43 through 50 represents five cards to be filed, numbered (1) through (5) shown in Column I. Each card is made up of the employee's name, a work assignment code number shown in parentheses, and the date of this assignment. The cards are to be filed according to the following rules:

First: File in alphabetical order.
Second: When two or more cards have the same employee's name, file according to the work assignment number, beginning with the lowest number.
Third: When two or more cards have the same employee's name and same assignment number, file according to the assignment date beginning with earliest date.

Column II shows the cards arranged in four different orders. Pick the answer (A, B, C, or D) in Column II which shows the cards arranged correctly according to the above filing rules.

SAMPLE QUESTION:

		Column I		Column II
(1)	Cluney	(486503)	6/17/07	A. 2, 3, 4, 1, 5
(2)	Roster	(246611)	5/10/06	B. 2, 5, 1, 3, 4
(3)	Altool	(711433)	10/15/07	C. 3, 2, 1, 4, 5
(4)	Cluney	(527610)	12/18/06	D. 3, 5, 1, 4, 2
(5)	Cluney	(486500)	4/8/07	

The CORRECT way to file the cards is:

(3)	Altool	(711433)	10/15/07
(5)	Cluney	(486500)	4/8/07
(1)	Cluney	(486503)	6/17/07
(4)	Cluney	(527610)	12/18/06
(2)	Roster	(246611)	5/10/06

The correct filing order is shown by the numbers in front of each name (3, 5, 1, 4, 2). The answer to the sample question is the letter in Column II in front of the numbers 3, 5, 1, 4, 2. This answer is D.

			Column I		Column II	
43.	(1)	Prichard	(013469)	4/6/06	A. 5, 4, 3, 2, 1	43.____
	(2)	Parks	(678941)	2/7/06	B. 1, 2, 5, 3, 4	
	(3)	Williams	(551467)	3/6/05	C. 2, 1, 5, 3, 4	
	(4)	Wilson	(551466)	8/9/02	D. 1, 5, 4, 3, 2	
	(5)	Stanhope	(300014)	8/9/02		
44.	(1)	Ridgeway	(623809)	8/11/06	A. 5, 1, 3, 4, 2	44.____
	(2)	Travers	(305439)	4/5/02	B. 5, 1, 3, 2, 4	
	(3)	Tayler	(818134)	7/5/03	C. 1, 5, 3, 2, 4	
	(4)	Travers	(305349)	5/6/05	D. 1, 5, 4, 2, 3	
	(5)	Ridgeway	(62309)	10/9/06		
45.	(1)	Jaffe	(384737)	2/19/06	A. 3, 5, 2, 4, 1	45.____
	(2)	Inez	(859176)	8/8/07	B. 3, 5, 2, 1, 4	
	(3)	Ingrahm	(946460)	8/6/04	C. 2, 3, 5, 1, 4	
	(4)	Karp	(256146)	5/5/05	D. 2, 3, 5, 4, 1	
	(5)	Ingrahm	(946460)	6/4/05		
46.	(1)	Marrano	(369421)	7/24/04	A. 1, 5, 3, 4, 2	46.____
	(2)	Marks	(652910)	2/23/06	B. 3, 5, 4, 2, 1	
	(3)	Netto	(556772)	3/10/07	C. 2, 4, 1, 5, 3	
	(4)	Marks	(652901)	2/17/07	D. 4, 2, 1, 5, 3	
	(5)	Netto	(556772)	6/17/05		
47.	(1)	Abernathy	(712467)	6/23/05	A. 5, 3, 1, 2, 4	47.____
	(2)	Acevedo	(680262)	6/23/03	B. 5, 4, 2, 3, 1	
	(3)	Aaron	(967647)	1/17/04	C. 1, 3, 5, 2, 4	
	(4)	Acevedo	(680622)	5/14/02	D. 2, 4, 1, 5, 3	
	(5)	Aaron	(967647)	4/1/00		

48.	(1)	Simon	(645219)	8/19/05	A. 4, 1, 2, 5, 3	48.____
	(2)	Simon	(645219)	9/2/03	B. 4, 5, 2, 1, 3	
	(3)	Simons	(645218)	7/7/05	C. 3, 5, 2, 1, 4	
	(4)	Simms	(646439)	10/12/06	D. 5, 1, 2, 3, 4	
	(5)	Simon	(645219)	10/16/02		
49.	(1)	Rappaport	(312230)	6/11/06	A. 4, 3, 1, 2, 5	49.____
	(2)	Rascio	(777510)	2/9/05	B. 4, 3, 1, 5, 2	
	(3)	Rappaport	(312230)	7/3/02	C. 3, 4, 1, 5, 2	
	(4)	Rapaport	(312330)	9/6/05	D. 5, 2, 4, 3, 1	
	(5)	Rascio	(777501)	7/7/05		
50.	(1)	Johnson	(843250)	6/8/02	A. 1, 3, 2, 4, 5	50.____
	(2)	Johnson	(843205)	4/3/05	B. 1, 3, 2, 5, 4	
	(3)	Johnson	(843205)	8/6/02	C. 3, 2, 1, 4, 5	
	(4)	Johnson	(843602)	3/8/06	D. 3, 2, 1, 5, 4	
	(5)	Johnson	(843602)	8/3/05		

KEY (CORRECT ANSWERS)

1.	D	11.	B	21.	C	31.	B	41.	C
2.	A	12.	A	22.	A	32.	B	42.	D
3.	C	13.	C	23.	D	33.	A	43.	C
4.	C	14.	C	24.	B	34.	C	44.	A
5.	C	15.	A	25.	D	35.	B	45.	C
6.	A	16.	D	26.	C	36.	A	46.	D
7.	B	17.	A	27.	B	37.	C	47.	A
8.	C	18.	C	28.	C	38.	B	48.	B
9.	D	19.	D	29.	A	39.	B	49.	B
10.	A	20.	B	30.	C	40.	B	50.	D

EXAMINATION SECTION

TEST 1

DIRECTIONS: Each question or incomplete statement is followed by several suggested answers or completions. Select the one that BEST answers the question or completes the statement. *PRINT THE LETTER OF THE CORRECT ANSWER IN THE SPACE AT THE RIGHT.*

Questions 1-5.

DIRECTIONS: Questions 1 through 5 consist of sentences, each of which contains one underlined word whose meaning you are to identify by marking your answer either A, B, C, or D.

EXAMPLE

Public employees should avoid <u>unethical</u> conduct.
The word unethical, as used in the sentence, means MOST NEARLY
A. fine B. dishonest C. polite D. sleepy
The correct answer is *dishonest* (B). Therefore, you should mark your answer B.

1. Employees who can produce a <u>considerable</u> amount of good work are very valuable. 1.____
The word *considerable*, as used in the sentence, means MOST NEARLY
A. large B. potential C. necessary D. frequent

2. No person should <u>assume</u> that he knows more than anyone else. 2.____
The word *assume*, as used in the sentence, means MOST NEARLY
A. verify B. hope C. suppose D. argue

3. The parties decided to <u>negotiate</u> through the night. 3.____
The word *negotiate*, as used in the sentence, means MOST NEARLY
A. suffer B. play C. think D. bargain

4. Employees who have <u>severe</u> emotional problems may create problems at work. 4.____
The word *severe*, as used in the sentence, means MOST NEARLY
A. serious B. surprising C. several D. common

5. Supervisors should try to be as <u>objective</u> as possible when dealing with subordinates. 5.____
The word *objective*, as used in the sentence, means MOST NEARLY
A. pleasant B. courteous C. fair D. strict

Questions 6-10.

DIRECTIONS: In each of Questions 6 through 10, one word is wrong because it is NOT in keeping with the intended meaning of the statement. First, decide which word is wrongly used; then select as your answer the right word which really belongs in its place.

EXAMPLE

The employee told ill and requested permission to leave early.
A. felt B. considered C. cried D. spoke
The word *"told"* is clearly wrong and not in keeping with the intended meaning of the quotation.
The word *"felt"* (A), however, would clearly convey the intended meaning of the sentence. Option A is correct. Your answer space, therefore, should be marked A.

6. Only unwise supervisors would deliberately overload their subordinates in order to create themselves look good. 6.____
A. delegate B. make C. reduce D. produce

7. In a democratic organization each employee is seen as a special individual kind of fair treatment. 7.____
A. granted B. denial C. perhaps D. deserving

8. In order to function the work flow in an office you should begin by identifying each important procedure being performed in that office. 8.____
A. uniformity B. study C. standards D. reward

9. A wise supervisor tries to save employees' time by simplifying forms or adding forms where possible. 9.____
A. taxing B. supervising C. eliminating D. protecting

10. A public agency, whenever it changes its program, should give requirements to the need for retraining its employees. 10.____
A. legislation B. consideration
C. permission D. advice

Questions 11-15.

DIRECTIONS: Questions 11 through 15 are to be answered ONLY on the basis of the reading passage preceding each question.

11. Things may not always be what they seem to be. Thus, the wise supervisor should analyze his problems and determine whether there is something there that does not meet the eye. For example, what may seem on the surface to be a personality clash between two subordinates may really be a problem of faulty organization, bad communication, or bad scheduling. 11.____

Which one of the following statements BEST supports this passage?
A. The wise supervisor should avoid personality clashes.
B. The smart supervisor should figure out what really is going on.
C. Bad scheduling is the result of faulty organization.
D. The best supervisor is the one who communicates effectively.

12. Some supervisors, under the pressure of meeting deadlines, become harsh and dictatorial to their subordinates. However, the supervisor most likely to be effective in meeting deadlines is one who absorbs or cushions pressures from above. 12.____
According to the passage, if a supervisor wishes to meet deadlines, it is MOST important that he
A. be informative to his superiors
B. encourage personal initiative among his subordinates
C. become harsh and dictatorial to his subordinates
D. protects his subordinates from pressures from above

13. When giving instructions, a supervisor must always make clear his meaning, leaving no room for misunderstanding. For example, a supervisor who tells a subordinate to do a task "as soon as possible" might legitimately be understood to mean either "it's top priority" or "do it when you can." 13.____
Which of the following statements is BEST supported by the passage?
A. Subordinates will attempt to avoid work by deliberately distorting instructions.
B. Instructions should be short, since brief instructions are the clearest.
C. Less educated subordinates are more likely to honestly misunderstand instructions.
D. A supervisor should give precise instructions that cannot be misinterpreted.

14. Practical formulas are often suggested to simplify what a supervisor should know and how he should behave, such as the four F's (be firm, fair, friendly, and factual). But such simple formulas are really broad principles, not necessarily specific guides in a real situation. 14.____
According to the passage, simple formulas for supervisory behavior
A. are superior to complicated theories and principles
B. not always of practical use in actual situations
C. useful only if they are fair and factual
D. would be better understood if written in clear language

15. Many management decisions are made far removed from the actual place of operations. Therefore, there is a great need for reliable reports and records and, the larger the organization, the greater is the need for such reports and records. 15.____
According to the passage, management decisions made far from the place of operations are
A. dependent to a great extent on reliable reports and records
B. sometimes in error because of the great distances involved

C. generally unreliable because of poor communications
D. generally more accurate than on-the-scene decisions

16. Assume that you have just been advanced to a supervisory administrative position and have been assigned as supervisor to a new office with subordinates you do not know. 16.____
The BEST way for you to establish good relations with these new subordinates would be to
A. announce that all actions of the previous supervisor are now cancelled
B. hold a meeting and warn them that you will not tolerate loafing on the job
C. reassign all your subordinates to new tasks on the theory that a thorough shake-up is good for morale
D. act fairly and show helpful interest in their work

17. One of your subordinates asks you to let her arrive at work 15 minutes later than usual but leave for the day 15 minutes later than she usually does. This is temporarily necessary, your subordinate states, because of early morning medication she must give her sick child. 17.____
Which of the following would be the MOST appropriate action for you to take?
A. Suggest to your subordinate that she choose another family doctor
B. Warn your subordinate that untruthful excuses are not acceptable
C. Tell your subordinate that you will consider the request and let her know very shortly
D. Deny the request since late arrival at work interferes with work performance

18. A young newly-hired employee asked his supervisor several times for advice on private financial matters. The supervisor commented, in a friendly manner, that he considered it undesirable to give such advice. 18.____
The supervisor's response was
A. *unwise*; the supervisor missed an opportunity to advise the employee on an important matter
B. *wise*; if the financial advice was wrong, it could damage the supervisor's relationship with the subordinate
C. *unwise*; the subordinate will take up the matter with his fellow workers and probably get poor advice
D. *wise*; the supervisor should never advise subordinates on any matter

19. Which of the following is the MOST justified reason for a supervisor to pay any serious attention to a subordinate's off-the-job behavior? The 19.____
A. subordinate's lifestyle is different from the supervisor's way of life
B. subordinate has become well-known as a serious painter of fine art
C. subordinate's work has become very poor as a result of his or her personal problems
D. subordinate is a reserved person who, at work, seldom speaks of personal matters

20. One of your subordinates complains to you that you assign him to the least pleasant jobs more often than anyone else. You are disturbed by this complaint since you believe you have always rotated such assignments on a fair basis. 20.____
Of the following, it would be BEST for you to tell the complaining subordinate that
   A. you will review your past assignment records and discuss the matter with him further
   B. complaints to supervisors are not the wise way to get ahead on the job
   C. disciplinary action will follow if the complaint is not justified
   D. he may be correct, but you do not have sufficient time to verify the complaint

21. Assume that you have called one of your subordinates into your office to talk about the increasing number of careless errors in her work. Until recently, this subordinate had been doing good work, but this is no longer so. Your subordinate does not seem to respond to your questions about the reason for her poor work. 21.____
In these circumstances, your NEXT step should be to tell her
   A. that her continued silence will result in severe disciplinary action
   B. to request an immediate transfer from your unit
   C. to return when she is ready to respond
   D. to be more open with you so that her work problem can be identified

22. Assume that you are given a complicated assignment with a tight deadline set by your superior. Shortly after you begin work you realize that, if you are to do a top quality job, you cannot possibly meet the deadline. 22.____
In these circumstances, what should be your FIRST course of action?
   A. Continue working as rapidly as possible, hoping that you will meet the deadline after all
   B. Request the assignment be given to an employee whom you believe works faster
   C. Advise your superior of the problem and see whether the deadline can be extended
   D. Advise your superior that the deadline cannot be met and, therefore, you will not start the job

23. Assume that a member of the public comes to you to complain about a long-standing practice of your agency. The complaint seems to be justified. 23.____
Which one of the following is the BEST way for you to handle this situation?
   A. Inform the complainant that you will have the agency practice looked into and that he will be advised of any action taken
   B. Listen politely, express sympathy, and state that you see no fault in the practice
   C. Express agreement with the practice on the ground that it has been in effect for many years
   D. Advise the complainant that things will work out well in good time

24. One of your subordinates tells you that he sees no reason for having departmental safety rules. 24.____
Which one of the following replies would be BEST for you to make?
    A. Rules are meant to be obeyed without question
    B. All types of rules are equally important
    C. Safety rules are meant to protect people from injury
    D. If a person is careful enough, he doesn't have to observe safety rules

25. Assume that a supervisor, when he issues instructions to his subordinates, usually names his superior as the source of these instructions. 25.____
This practice is GENERALLY
    A. *wise*, since if things go wrong, the subordinates will know whom to blame
    B. *unwise*, since it may give the subordinates the impression that the supervisor doesn't really support the instructions
    C. *wise*, since it clearly invites the subordinates to go to higher authority if they don't like the instructions

KEY (CORRECT ANSWERS)

1. A
2. C
3. D
4. A
5. C
6. B
7. D
8. B
9. C
10. B
11. B
12. D
13. D
14. B
15. A
16. D
17. C
18. B
19. C
20. A
21. D
22. C
23. A
24. C
25. B

TEST 2

DIRECTIONS: Each question or incomplete statement is followed by several suggested answers or completions. Select the one that BEST answers the question or completes the statement. *PRINT THE LETTER OF THE CORRECT ANSWER IN THE SPACE AT THE RIGHT.*

1. An office aide is assigned as a receptionist in a busy office. The office aide often has stretches of idle time between visitors. 1.____
In this situation, the supervisor should
   A. give the receptionist non-urgent clerical jobs which can quickly be done at the reception desk
   B. offer all office aides an opportunity to volunteer for this assignment
   C. eliminate the receptionist assignment
   D. continue the arrangement unchanged, because receptionist duties are so important nothing should interfere with them

2. A supervisor can MOST correctly assume that an employee is not performing up to his usual standard when the employee does not handle a task as skillfully as 2.____
   A. do other employees who have received less training
   B. do similar employees having comparable work experience
   C. he has handled it in several recent instances
   D. the supervisor himself could handle it

3. Assume that you receive a suggestion that you direct all the typists in a typing pool to complete the identical quantity of work each day. 3.____
For you to adopt this suggestion would be
   A. *advisable*; it will demonstrate the absence of supervisory favoritism
   B *advisable*; all employees in a given title should be treated identically
   C. *inadvisable*; a supervisor should decide on work standards without interference from others
   D. *inadvisable*; it ignores variations in specific assignments and individual skills

4. A certain supervisor encouraged her subordinates to tell her if they become aware of possible job problems. 4.____
This practice is good MAINLY because
   A. early awareness of job problems allows more time for seeking solutions
   B. such expected job problems may not develop
   C. the supervisor will be able to solve the job problem without consulting other people
   D. the supervisor will be able to place responsibility for poor work

5. Some supervisors will discuss with a subordinate how he is doing on the job only when indicating his mistakes or faults. 5.____
Which of the following is the MOST likely result of such a practice?
   A. The subordinate will become discouraged and frustrated.
   B. Management will set work standards too low.

C. The subordinate will be favorably impressed by the supervisor's frankness.
D. Supervisors will avoid creating any impression of favoritism.

6. A supervisor calls in a subordinate he supervises to discuss the subordinate's annual work performance, indicating his work deficiencies and also praising his job strengths. The subordinate nods his head as if in agreement with his supervisor's comments on both his strengths and weaknesses, but actually says nothing, even after the supervisor has completed his comments. 6.____
At this point, the supervisor should
A. end the session and assume that the subordinate agrees completely with the evaluation
B. end the session, since all the subordinate's good and bad points have been identified
C. ask the supervisor whether the criticism is justified, and, if so, what he, the supervisor, can do to help
D. thank the subordinate for being so fair-minded in accepting the criticism in a positive manner

7. The successful supervisor is often one who gives serious attention to his subordinates' needs for job satisfaction. 7.____
A supervisor who believes this statement is MOST likely to
A. treat all subordinates in an identical manner, irrespective of individual differences
B. permit each subordinate to perform his work as he wishes, within reasonable limits
C. give all subordinates both criticism and praise in equal measure
D. provide each subordinate with as much direct supervision as possible

8. Assume that you are supervising seven subordinates and have been asked by your superior to prepare an especially complex report due today. Its completion will take the rest of the day. You break down the assignment into simple parts and give a different part to each subordinate. 8.____
If you were to explain the work of each subordinate to more than one subordinate, your decision would be
A. *wise*; this would prevent boredom
B. *unwise*; valuable time would be lost
C. *wise*; your subordinates would become well-rounded
D. *unwise*; your subordinates would lose their competitive spirit

9. Suppose that an office associate whom you supervise has given you a well-researched report on a problem in an area in which he is expert. However, the report lacks solutions or recommendations. You know this office associate to be fearful of stating his opinions. 9.____
In these circumstances, you should tell him that
A. you will seek recommendations on the problem from other, even if less expert, office associates
B. his work is satisfactory, in hope of arousing him to greater assertiveness

C. you need his advice and expertise, to help you reach a decision on the problem
D. his uncooperative behavior leaves you no choice but to speak to your superior

10. If a supervisor wishes to have the work of his unit completed on schedule, it is usually MOST important to 10.____
A. avoid listening to employees' complaints, thereby discouraging dissatisfaction
B. perform much of the work himself, since he is generally more capable
C. observe employees continuously, so they do not slacken their efforts
D. set up the work carefully, then stay informed as to how it is moving

11. Of the following agencies, the one MOST likely to work out a proposed budget close to its real needs is 11.____
A. a newly-created agency staffed by inexperienced administrators
B. funded with a considerable amount of money
C. an existing agency which intends to install new, experimental systems for doing its work
D. an existing agency which can base its estimate on its experience during the past few years

12. Assume that you are asked to prepare a report on the expected costs and benefits of a proposed new program to be installed in your office. However, you are aware that certain factors are not really measurable in dollars and cents. 12.____
As a result, you should
A. identify the non-measurable factors and state why they are important
B. assign a fixed money value to all factors that are not really measurable
C. recommend that programs containing non-measurable factors should be dropped
D. assume that the non-measurable factors are really unimportant

13. Assume that you are asked for your opinion as to the necessity for hiring more employees to perform certain revenue-producing work in your office. 13.____
The information that you will MOST likely need in giving an informed opinion is
A. whether public opinion would favor hiring additional employees
B. an estimate of the probable additional revenue compared with the additional personnel costs
C. the total cost of all city operations in contrast to all city revenues
D. the method by which present employees would be selected for promotion in an expanded operation

14. The MOST reasonable number of subordinate for a supervisor to have is BEST determined by the 14.____
A. average number of subordinates other supervisors have
B. particular responsibilities given to the supervisor
C. supervisor's educational background
D. personalities of the subordinates assigned to the supervisor

15. Most subordinates would need less supervision if they knew what they were supposed to do. 15.____
An ESSENTIAL first step in fixing in subordinates' minds exactly what is required of them is to
   A. require that supervisors be firm in their supervision of subordinates
   B. encourage subordinates to determine their own work standards
   C. encourage subordinates to submit suggestions to improve procedures
   D. standardize and simplify procedures and logically schedule activities

16. Assume that you have been asked to recommend an appropriate office layout to correspond with a just completed office reorganization. 16.____
Which of the following is it MOST advisable to recommend?
   A. Allocate most of the space for traffic flow
   B. Use the center area only for traffic flow
   C. Situate close to each other those units whose work is closely related
   D. Group in an out-of-the-way corner the supply and file cabinets

17. Although an organization chart will illustrate the formal structure of an agency, it will seldom show a true picture of its actual workings. 17.____
Which of the following BEST explains this statement?
Organization charts
   A. are often prepared by employees who may exaggerate their own importance
   B. usually show titles and sometimes names rather than the actual contacts and movements between employees
   C. are likely to discourage the use of official titles, and in so doing promote greater freedom in human relations
   D. usually show the informal arrangements and dealings between employees

18. Assume that a supervisor of a large unit has a variety of tasks to perform, and that he gives each of his subordinates just one set of tasks to do. He never rotates subordinates from one set of tasks to another. 18.____
Which one of the following is the MOST likely advantage to be gained by this practice?
   A. Each subordinate will get to know all the tasks of the unit.
   B. The subordinate will be encouraged to learn all they can about all the unit's tasks.
   C. Each subordinate will become an expert in his particular set of tasks.
   D. The subordinates will improve their opportunities for promotion.

19. Listed below are four steps commonly used in trying to solve administrative problems. These four steps are not listed in the order in which they normally would be taken. If they were listed in the proper order, which step should be taken FIRST? 19.____
   I. Choosing the most practical solution to the problem
   II. Analyzing the essential facts about the problem
   III. Correctly identifying the problem
   IV. Following up to see if the solution chosen really works

The CORRECT answer is:
A. III B. I C. II D. IV

20. Assume that another agency informally tells you that most of your agency's reports are coming to them with careless errors made by many of your office aides. 20.____
Which one of the following is MOST likely to solve this problem?
A. Require careful review of all outgoing reports by the supervisors of the office aides
B. Request the other agency to make necessary corrections whenever such errors come to their attention
C. Ask the other agency to submit a written report on this situation
D. Establish a small unit to review all reports received from other agencies

21. Assume that you supervise an office which gets two kinds of work. One kind is high-priority and must be done within two days. The other kind of work must be done within two weeks. 21.____
Which one of the following instructions would be MOST reasonable for you to give to your subordinates in this office?
A. If a backlog builds up during the day, clean the backlog up first, regardless of priority
B. Spend half the day doing priority work and the other half doing non-priority work
C. Generally do the priority work first as soon as it is received
D. Usually do the work in the order in which it comes in, priority or non-priority

22. An experienced supervisor should do advance planning of his subordinates' work assignments and schedules. 22.____
Which one of the following is the BEST reason for such advance planning?
It
A. enables the supervisor to do less supervision
B. will assure the assignment of varied duties
C. will make certain a high degree of discipline among subordinates
D. helps make certain that essential operations are adequately covered

23. Agencies are required to evaluate the performance of their employees. 23.____
Which one of the following would generally be POOR evaluation practice by an agency rater?
The rater
A. regularly observes the performance of the employee being rated
B. in evaluating the employee, acquaints himself with the employee's job
C. uses objective standards in evaluating the employee being rated
D. uses different standards in evaluating men and women

24. A good supervisor should have a clear idea of the quantity and quality of his subordinates' work. 24.____
Which one of the following sources would normally provide a supervisor with the LEAST reliable information about a subordinate's work performance?
   A. Discussion with a friend of the subordinate
   B. Comments by other supervisors who have worked recently with the subordinate
   C. Opinions of fellow workers who work closely with the subordinate on a daily basis
   D. Comparison with work records of others doing similar work during the same period of time

25. In order to handle the ordinary work of an office, a supervisor sets up standard work procedures. 25.____
The MOST likely benefit of this is to reduce the need to
   A. motivate employees to do superior work
   B. rethink what has to be done every time a routine matter comes up
   C. keep record and write reports
   D. change work procedures as new situations come up

KEY (CORRECT ANSWERS)

1.	A	11.	D
2.	C	12.	A
3.	D	13.	B
4.	A	14.	B
5.	A	15.	D
6.	C	16.	C
7.	B	17.	B
8.	B	18.	C
9.	C	19.	A
10.	D	20.	A

21.	C
22.	D
23.	D
24.	A
25.	B

EXAMINATION SECTION

TEST 1

DIRECTIONS: Each question or incomplete statement is followed by several suggested answers or completions. Select the one that BEST answers the question or completes the statement. *PRINT THE LETTER OF THE CORRECT ANSWER IN THE SPACE AT THE RIGHT.*

1. An executive assigns A, the head of a staff unit, to devise plans for reducing the delay in submittal of reports by a local agency headed by C. The reports are under the supervision of C's subordinate line official B with whom A is to deal directly. In his investigation, A finds: (1) the reasons for the delay; and (2) poor practices which have either been overlooked or condoned by line official B. 1.____
   Of the following courses of action A could take, the BEST one would be to
   A. develop recommendations with line official B with regard to reducing the delay and correcting the poor practice and then report fully to his own executive
   B. discuss the findings with C in an attempt to correct the situation before making any formal report on the poor practices
   C. report both findings to his executive, attaching the explanation offered by C
   D. report to his executive on the first finding and discuss the second in a friendly way with line official B
   E. report the first finding to his executive, ignoring the second until his opinion is requested

2. Drafts of a proposed policy, prepared by a staff committee, are circulated to ten member of the field staff of the organization by route slips with a request for comments within two weeks. Two members of the field staff make extensive comments, four offer editorial suggestions, and the remainder make minor favorable comments. Shortly after, it found that the statement needs considerable revision by the field staff. 2.____
   Of the following possible reasons for the original failure of the field staff to identify difficulties, the MOST likely is that the
   A. field staff did not take sufficient time to review the manual
   B. field staff had not been advised of the type of contribution expected
   C. low morale of the field staff prevented their showing interest
   D. policy statement was too advanced for the staff
   E. staff committee was not sufficiently representative

3. Operator participation in management improvement work is LEAST likely to 3.____
   A. assure the use of best available management technique
   B. overcome the stigma of the outside expert
   C. place responsibility for improvement in the person who knows the job best
   D. simplify installation
   E. take advantage of the desire of most operators to seek self-improvement

4. In general, the morale of workers in an agency is MOST frequently and MOST significantly affected by the 4.____
   A. agency policies of organizational structure and operational procedures
   B. distance of the employee's job from his home community
   C. fringe benefits
   D. number of opportunities for advancement
   E. relationship with supervisors

5. Of the following, the PRIMARY function of a work distribution chart is to 5.____
   A. analyze the soundness of existing divisions of labor
   B. eliminate the unnecessary clerical detail
   C. establish better supervisory techniques
   D. simplify work methods
   E. weed out core functions

6. In analyzing a process chart, which one of the following should be asked FIRST? 6.____
   A. How B. When C. Where D. Who E. Why

7. Which one of the following is NOT an advantage of the interview method of collecting data? It 7.____
   A. enables interviewer to judge the person interviewed on such matters as general attitude, knowledge, etc.
   B. helps build up personal relations for later installation of changes
   C. is a flexible method that can be adjusted to changing circumstances
   D. permits the obtaining of *off the record* information
   E. produces more accurate information than other methods

8. Which one of the following may be defined as a *regularly recurring appraisal of the manner in which all elements of agency management are being carried out*? 8.____
   A. Functional survey B. Operations audit
   C. Organization survey D. Over-all survey
   E. Reconnaissance survey

9. An analysis of the flow of work in a department should begin with the _____ work. 9.____
   A. major routine B. minor routine C. supervisory
   D. technical E. unusual

10. Which method would MOST likely be used to get first-hand information on complaints from the public? 10.____
   A. Study of correspondence
   B. Study of work volume
   C. Tracing specific transactions through a series of steps
   D. Tracing use of forms
   E. Worker desk audit

11. People will generally produce the MOST if 11.____
    A. management exercises close supervision over the work
    B. there is strict discipline in the group
    C. they are happy in their work
    D. they feel involved in their work
    E. they follow *the one best way*

12. The normal analysis of which chart listed below is MOST closely related to organizational analysis? _____ chart. 12.____
    A. Layout
    B. Operation
    C. Process
    D. Work count
    E. Work distribution

13. The work count would be LEAST helpful in accomplishing which one of the following? 13.____
    A. Demonstrating personnel needs
    B. Improving the sequence of steps
    C. Measuring the value of a step
    D. Spotting bottlenecks
    E. Stimulating interest in work

14. Which one of the following seems LEAST useful as a guide in interviewing an employee in a procedure and methods survey? 14.____
    A. Explaining who you are and the purpose of your visit
    B. Having a general plan of what you intend to get from the interview
    C. Listening carefully and not interrupting
    D. Trying out his reactions to your ideas for improvements
    E. Trying to analyze his reasons for saying what he says

15. Which one of the following is an advantage of the questionnaire method of gathering facts as compared with the interview method? 15.____
    A. Different people may interpret the questions differently
    B. Less *off the record* information is given
    C. More time may be taken in order to give exact answers
    D. Personal relationships with the people involved are not established
    E. There is less need for follow-up

16. Which one of the following is generally NOT an advantage of the personal observation method of gathering facts? It 16.____
    A. enables staff to use *off the record* information if personally observed
    B. helps in developing valid recommendations
    C. helps the person making the observation acquire *know how* valuable for later installation and follow-up
    D. is economical in time and money
    E. may turn up other problems in need of solution

17. Which of the following would MOST often be the best way to minimize resistance to change? 17.____
    A. Break the news about the change gently to the people affected
    B. Increase the salary of the people affected by the change
    C. Let the people concerned participate at the decision to change

D. Notify all people concerned with the change, both orally and in writing
E. Stress the advantages of the new system

18. The functional organization chart 18.____
A. does not require periodic revision
B. includes a description of the duties of each organization segment
C. includes positions and titles for each organization segment
D. is the simplest type of organization chart
E. is used primarily by newly established agencies

19. The principle of span of control has frequently been said to be in conflict with the 19.____
A. principle of unity of command
B. principle that authority should be commensurate with responsibility
C. principle that like functions should be grouped into one unit
D. principle that the number of levels between the top of an organization and the bottom should be small
E. scalar principle

20. If an executive delegates to his subordinates authority to handle problems of a routine nature for which standard solutions have been established, he may expect that 20.____
A. fewer complaint will be received
B. he has made it more difficult for his subordinates to solve these problems
C. he has opened the way for confusion in his organization
D. there will be a lack of consistency in the methods applied to the solution of these problems
E. these routine problems will be handled efficiently and he will have more time for other non-routine work

21. Which of the following would MOST likely be achieved by a change in the basic organization structure from the *process* or *functional* type to the *purpose* or *product* type? 21.____
A. Easier recruitment of personnel in a tight labor market
B. Fixing responsibility at a lower level in the organization
C. Greater centralization
D. Greater economy
E. Greater professional development

22. Usually the MOST difficult problem in connection with a major reorganization is 22.____
A. adopting a pay plan to fit the new structure
B. bringing the organization manual up-to-date
C. determining the new organization structure
D. gaining acceptance of the new plan by the higher level employees
E. gaining acceptance of the new plan by the lower level employees

23. Which of the following statements MOST accurately describes the work of the chiefs of MOST staff divisions in departments? 23.____
Chiefs
   A. focus more on getting the job done than on how it is done
   B. are mostly interested in short-range results
   C. nearly always advise but rarely advise
   D. usually command or control but rarely advise
   E. provide service to the rest of the organization and/or assist the chief executive in planning and controlling operations

24. In determining the type of organization structure of an enterprise, the one factor that might be given relatively greater weight in a small organization than in a larger organization of the same nature is the 24.____
   A. geographical location of the enterprise
   B. individual capabilities of incumbents
   C. method of financing to be employed
   D. size of the area served
   E. type of activity engaged in

25. Functional foremanship differs MOST markedly from generally accepted principle of administration in that it advocates 25.____
   A. an unlimited span of control
   B. less delegation of responsibility
   C. more than one supervisor for an employee
   D. nonfunctional organization
   E. substitution of execution for planning

KEY (CORRECT ANSWERS)

1.	A	11.	D
2.	B	12.	E
3.	A	13.	B
4.	E	14.	D
5.	A	15.	C
6.	E	16.	D
7.	E	17.	C
8.	B	18.	B
9.	A	19.	D
10.	A	20.	E

21.	B
22.	D
23.	E
24.	B
25.	C

TEST 2

DIRECTIONS: Each question or incomplete statement is followed by several suggested answers or completions. Select the one that BEST answers the question or completes the statement. *PRINT THE LETTER OF THE CORRECT ANSWER IN THE SPACE AT THE RIGHT.*

1. Decentralization of the authority to make decisions is a necessary result of increased complexity in an organization, but for the sake of efficiency and coordination of operations, such decentralization must be planned carefully. A good general rule is that 1.____
   A. any decision should be made at the lowest possible point in the organization where all the information and competence necessary for a sound decision are available
   B. any decision should be made at the highest possible point in the organization, thus guaranteeing the best decision
   C. any decision should be made at the lowest possible point in the organization, but always approved by management
   D. any decision should be made by management and referred to the proper subordinate for comment
   E. no decision should be made by any individual in the organization without approval by a superior

2. One drawback of converting a conventional consecutive filing system to a terminal digit filing system for a large installation is that 2.____
   A. conversion would be expensive in time and manpower
   B. conversion would prevent the proper use of recognized numeric classification systems, such as the Dewey decimal, in classifying files material
   C. responsibility for proper filing cannot be pinpointed in the terminal digit system
   D. the terminal digit system requires considerably more space than a normal filing system

3. The basic filing system that would ordinarily be employed in a large administrative headquarters unit is the _____ file system. 3.____
   A alphabetic
   B. chronological
   C. mnemonic
   D. retention
   E. subject classification

4. A records center is of benefit in a records management program PRIMARILY because 4.____
   A. all the records of the organization are kept in one place
   B. inactive records can be stored economically in less expense storage areas
   C. it provides a place where useless records can be housed at little or no cost to the organization

D. obsolete filing and storage equipment can be utilized out of view of the public
E. records analysts can examine an organization's files without affecting the unit's operation or upsetting the supervisors

5. In examining a number of different forms to see whether any could be combined or eliminated, which of the following would one be MOST likely to use? 5.____
A. Forms analysis sheet of recurring data
B. Forms control log
C. Forms design and approval request
D. Forms design and guide sheet
E. Numerical file

6. The MOST important reason for control of *bootleg* forms is that 6.____
A. they are more expensive than authorized forms
B. they are usually poorly designed
C. they can lead to unnecessary procedures
D. they cannot be reordered as easily as authorized terms
E. violation of rules and regulations should not be allowed

7. With a box design of a form, the caption title or question to be answered should be located in the _____ of the box. 7.____
A. center at the bottom
B. center at the top
C. lower left corner
D. lower right corner
E. upper left corner

8. A two-part snapout form would be MOST properly justified if 8.____
A. it is a cleaner operation
B. it is prepared ten times a week
C. it saves time in preparation
D. it is to be filled out by hand rather than by typewriter
E. proper registration is critical

9. When deciding whether or not to approve a request for a new form, which reference is normally MOST pertinent? 9.____
A. Alphabetical Forms File
B. Functional Forms File
C. Numerical Forms File
D. Project Completion Report
E. Records Retention Data

10. Which of the following statements BEST explains the significance of the famed Hawthorne Plant experiments? 10.____
They showed that
A. a large span of control leads to more production than a small span of control
B. morale has no relationship to production
C. personnel counseling is of relatively little importance in a going organization

D. the special attention received by a group in an experimental situation has a greater impact on production than changes in working conditions
E. there is a direct relationship between the amount of illumination and production

11. Which of the following would most often NOT result from a highly efficient management control system? 11.____
A. Facilitation of delegation
B. Highlighting of problem areas
C. Increase in willingness of people to experiment or to take calculated risks
D. Provision of an objective test of new ideas or new methods and procedures
E. Provision of information useful for revising objectives, programs, and operations

12. The PERT system is a 12.____
A. method for laying out office space on a modular basis utilizing prefabricated partitions
B. method of motivating personnel to be continuously alert and to improve their appearance
C. method of program planning and control using a network or flow plan
D. plan for expanding reporting techniques
E. simplified method of cost accounting

13. The term *management control* is MOST frequently used to mean 13.____
A. an objective and unemotional approach by management
B. coordinating the efforts of all parts of the organization
C. evaluation of results in relation to plan
D. giving clear, precise orders to subordinates
E. keeping unions from making managerial decisions

14. Which one of the following factors has the MOST bearing on the frequency with which a control report should be made? 14.____
A. Degree of specialization of the work
B. Degree of variability in activities
C. Expense of the report
D. Number of levels of supervision
E. Number of personnel involved

15. The value of statistical records is MAINLY dependent upon the 15.____
A. method of presenting the material
B. number of items used
C. range of cases sampled
D. reliability of the information used
E. time devoted to compiling the material

16. When a supervisor delegates an assignment, he should 16.____
    A. delegate his responsibility for the assignment
    B. make certain that the assignment is properly performed
    C. participate in the beginning and final stages of the assignment
    D. retail all authority needed to complete the assignment
    E oversee all stages of the assignment

17. Assume that the department in which you are employed has never given official sanction to a mid-afternoon coffee break. Some bureaus have it and others do not. In the latter case, some individuals merely absent themselves for about 15 minutes at 3 P.M. while others remain on the job despite the fatigue which seems to be common among all employees in this department at that time. 17.____
    The course of action which you should recommend, if possible, is to
    A. arrange a schedule of mid-afternoon coffee breaks for all employees
    B. forbid all employees to take a mid-afternoon coffee break
    C. permit each bureau to decide for itself whether or not it will have a coffee break
    D. require all employees who wish a coffee break to take a shorter lunch period
    E. arrange a poll to discover the consensus of the department

18. The one of the following which is LEAST important in the management of a suggestion program is 18.____
    A. giving awards which are of sufficient value to encourage competition
    B. securing full support from the department's officers and executives
    C. publicizing the program and the awards given
    D. holding special conferences to analyze and evaluate some of the suggestions needed
    E. providing suggestion boxes in numerous locations

19. The one of the following which is MOST likely to decrease morale is 19.____
    A. insistence on strict adherence to safety rules
    B. making each employee responsible for the tidiness of his work area
    C. overlooking evidence of hostility between groups of employees
    D. strong, aggressive leadership
    E. allocating work on the basis of personal knowledge of the abilities and interests of the member of the department

20. Assume that a certain office procedure has been standard practice for many years. 20.____
    When a new employee asks why this particular procedure is followed, the supervisor should FIRST
    A. explain that everyone does it that way
    B. explain the reason for the procedure
    C. inform him that it has always been done that way in that particular office
    D. tell him to try it for a while before asking questions
    E. tell him he has never thought about it that way

21. Several employees complain informally to their supervisor regarding some new procedures which have been instituted. 21.____
The supervisor should IMMEDIATELY
A. explain that management is responsible
B. state frankly that he had nothing to do with it
C. refer the matter to the methods analyst
D. tell the employees to submit their complaint as a formal grievance
E. investigate the complaint

22. A new employee asks his supervisor how he is doing. Actually, he is not doing well in some phases of the job, but it is felt that he will learn in time. 22.____
The BEST response for the supervisor to make is:
A. Some things you are doing well, and in others I am sure you will improve.
B. Wait until the end of your probation period when we will discuss this matter.
C. You are not doing too well.
D. You are doing very well.
E. I'll be able to tell you when I go over your record.

23. The PRINCIPAL aim of a supervisor is to 23.____
A. act as liaison between employee and management
B. get the work done
C. keep up morale
D. train his subordinates
E. become chief of the department

24. When the work of two bureaus must be coordinated, direct contact between the subordinates in each bureau who are working on the problem is 24.____
A. *bad*, because it violates the chain of command
B. *bad*, because they do not have authority to make decisions
C. *good*, because it enable quicker results
D. *good*, because it relieves their superiors of any responsibilities
E. *bad*, because they may work at cross purposes

25. Of the following, the organization defect which can be ascertained MOST readily merely by analyzing an accurate and well-drawn organization chart is 25.____
A. ineffectiveness of an activity
B. improper span of control
C. inappropriate assignment of functions
D. poor supervision
E. unlawful delegation of authority

KEY (CORRECT ANSWERS)

1. A
2. A
3. E
4. B
5. A

6. C
7. E
8. E
9. B
10. D

11. C
12. C
13. C
14. B
15. D

16. B
17. A
18. E
19. C
20. B

21. E
22. A
23. B
24. C
25. B

EXAMINATION SECTION
TEST 1

DIRECTIONS: Each question or incomplete statement is followed by several suggested answers or completions. Select the one that BEST answers the question or completes the statement. *PRINT THE LETTER OF THE CORRECT ANSWER IN THE SPACE AT THE RIGHT.*

1. You are assigned to form a new unit to compile data which is to facilitate an executive in decision-making. 1.____
In planning the organization of this unit, the question to be answered FIRST is:

   A. What interpretations are likely to be made of the data by the executive in making a decision?
   B. At what point in the decision-making process will the data be most usefully introduced?
   C. What type of data is needed by the executive in his area of decision-making?
   D. What criteria will the executive use to evaluate the data?

2. The extent of effective decentralization within an organization is INVERSELY related to the 2.____

   A. size of the organization
   B. availability of sufficient competent personnel
   C. physical dispersion of the organization's activities
   D. effectiveness of communication within the organization

3. *The tasks of coordination, supervision, and control are likely to become more complicated as the specialization of an organization increases.* 3.____
This statement is GENERALLY

   A. *false;* better performance of these tasks is likely to follow from the detailed attention given to particular problems
   B. *false;* the proportion of specialized personnel is small in proportion to total personnel
   C. *true;* the increased interrelationships arising from increased specialization are sources of potential friction
   D. *true;* the specialist tends to resent direction from superiors who are not specialists

4. The distinctive feature between a method and a procedure may BEST be illustrated by a 4.____

   A. series of procedures comprising a method
   B. series of related methods performed usually by one person constituting a procedure
   C. procedure comprised of a series of related methods
   D. procedure encompassing a range more limited than that of a method

5. As part of your duties to analyze operating practices, you make a tour of a unit during which you talk to the employees about work methods, problems, and other pertinent topics. Such informal data gathering is often incomplete or inaccurate. At a later meeting with the unit supervisor, you question him about the information you have gathered, but he is unable to answer the questions immediately. He asks to accompany you on another tour of his unit and answer the questions on the spot. Explaining that employees will be reluctant to speak up in the presence of a supervisor, you refuse. 5.____
The situation you have created may BEST be described as a violation of the principle of organization called

A. delegation of authority
B. specialization of work
C. span of control
D. unity of command

6. A person desiring greater status and income in municipal government must, with few exceptions, move into the supervisory ranks. When he does, he will encounter certain changes in attitudes and relationships to which he must make satisfactory adjustments. His rise will create a degree of hostility and natural jealousy among his colleagues who have not tried to improve their situation or who have tried and failed. In a sense, too, he is forced upon the group he will supervise because under normal civil service practice, the group has little to say in his appointment. 6.____
A subtle change takes place also in his social situation; he must be in contact with his subordinates but he cannot be part of them, otherwise he yields a basic obligation to management, of which he is a part.
The MOST important conclusion to be made from this statement is that

A. a manager should limit his contacts with subordinates to a minimum
B. he must plan to advance himself further
C. he should isolate himself from the work of the supervised group
D. he must subordinate personnel popularity to the interest of the organization

7. A budget that itemizes expenditure estimates by detailing materials to be purchased, equipment to be maintained, salaries to be paid, etcetera, is known as a ______ budget. 7.____

A. performance
B. capital
C. line-item
D. program

8. Organizational activities for which there are no allocated funds available are financed from the ______ funds. 8.____

A. special revenue
B. sinking
C. general
D. special assessment

9. One of the real revolutions in public administration during the last half-century is the growth in importance of the budget as a planning and control instrument. Several trends account for this growing importance. Which of the following is NOT one of these trends? 9.____

A. Rapid growth of the urban population
B. The cheapening of the dollar
C. The improved standards of living
D. Full employment

10. The position classifying bureau of the personnel agency is normally NOT responsible for 10.____

A. allocating individuals to classes
B. assigning titles to classes of positions
C. establishing minimum qualifications for positions
D. determining which positions are necessary

11. Which of the following statements concerning a job analysis for position classification is FALSE? 11.____

A. It is a study of the person who is to occupy the job.
B. Time and motion studies may be used.
C. It may be used in establishing rates of compensation.
D. It is often done by staff authority.

12. Which of the following is considered to be an ESSENTIAL element of classifying a position? 12.____

A. Number of positions similar to the one being classified
B. Determination of salary to be paid for position
C. Comparison of the position with similar and related positions
D. Evaluation of the skills demanded by the position

13. The LEAST important objective of devising a service rating system is 13.____

A. validating selection procedures
B. improving quality of supervision
C. encouraging the development of employee performance
D. furnishing the basis of formulating a position classification plan

Questions 14-15.

DIRECTIONS: Questions 14 and 15 are to be answered in accordance with the following statement.

The process of validating a factual proposition is quite distinct from the process of validating a value judgment. The former is validated by its agreement with the facts, the latter by human authority.

14. According to the above statement, the one of the following methods which is MOST acceptable for determining whether or not a proposition is factually correct is to 14.____

A. prove that a related proposition is factually correct
B. derive it logically from accepted assumptions
C. show that it will lead to desired results
D. compare it with experience

15. Assuming that the above statement is correct, the theory that the correctness of all ethical propositions can be tested empirically is 15.____

A. *correct;* testing empirically is validating by agreement with facts
B. *incorrect;* ethical propositions are value judgments
C. *correct;* ethical propositions are based on rational hypotheses
D. *incorrect;* a factual proposition is validated by its agreement with facts

16. The rejection of the theory of inverse probability was, for a time, wrongly taken to imply that we cannot draw, from knowledge of a sample, inferences respecting the corresponding population. Such a view would entirely deny validity to all experimental science. According to the above statement, 16.____

A. the theory of inverse probability cannot be applied to an entire population
B. making deductions from a sample is consistent with experimental science
C. making deductions from a sample is inconsistent with experimental science
D. the theory of Inverse probability is based on the study of samples

17. May I point out that if technical employees are given assignments only in their special fields, there will be an immediate gain in conserving special skills. And, if we are to make optimum use of the abilities of the technical employees, it is necessary that these skills be conserved. 17.____
Assuming that this analysis is correct, it follows that

A. if we are not making optimum use of the abilities of technical employees, we have been giving technical employees assignments outside of their special fields
B. we are making optimum use of the abilities of technical employees if we conserve special skills
C. we are making optimum use of the abilities of technical employees if we give them assignments only in their special fields
D. we are not making optimum use of the abilities of technical employees if we give them assignments outside of their special fields

18. *It is less costly to replace old equipment than to repair it.* 18.____
Which of the following statements tends to prove this hypothesis MOST conclusively?

A. The repair of old equipment is frequently as costly as the purchase of new equipment.
B. Continuance in service of old equipment is at least as costly as its replacement by new equipment.
C. The replacement of old equipment is more desirable than its repair.
D. The cost for repairing old equipment is not a one-time cost, while the cost of new equipment is a one-time cost.

19. *An increasing birth rate will be followed by an increased school registration.* 19.____
On the basis of this statement *only,* it would be MOST accurate to state that

A. school registration does not change during a period with a level birth rate
B. an increasing school registration is preceded by a period with an increasing birth rate
C. a period with an increasing birth rate is sometimes followed by a decreasing school registration
D. a period with a decreasing birth rate is sometimes followed by a decreasing school registration

20. It is generally agreed that the *face-to-face* method of communicating is the most effective from a supervisor's standpoint. 20.____
This is true PRIMARILY because

A. the attitude of the recipient can be accurately appraised
B. it provides a two-way channel of expression which results in clarification of ideas
C. it is illustrative of the extremely desirable supervisory technique known as the *democratic approach*
D. it brings the supervisor closer to the actual level of operation

Questions 21-25.

DIRECTIONS: Questions 21 through 25 contain incorrectly used words which change the meaning of the statement. Identify the word in the statement that is incorrect and select the choice that would make the sentence correct.

21. Lack of employee input in the case of training often exists, but is frequently dealt with in evaluation of the training effort. Failure to deal with as important a factor as this can be ruinous to the training effort. 21.____

A. Seldom B. Margin C. Ancillary D. Contributory

22. It is a fallacy that policies generated at the top of the hierarchy are often not acceptable to those on the lower levels, particularly in the case of blue-collar workers among whom the rewards and sanctions of the union or members of the immediate social group are more impelling than the rewards or sanctions available to management. 22.____

A. Parologism
B. Truism
C. Commands
D. Undetermined

23. Basically, an organization develops when employees in it have rather free control over their behavior within the organization, when the philosophy of the organization is that maximum interpersonal interplay through a minimum number of hierarchical levels is desirable, and when a person traditionally called a *trainer* performs an integrating function. 23.____

A. Instinctively
B. Total
C. Flat
D. Strong

24. In gaining cooperation in human relations, the one who would influence must often foster his own ego and fertilize and feed that of the one who is to be influenced. 24.____

A. Lassitude B. Emulate C. Suppress D. Implant

25. In the United States, in general, we have been criticized for our emphasis upon physical, materialistic, and economic goals. These are still important, but the trends point toward the more complex, or appreciation of the beautiful, as for example in the architecture of our new factories and colors in the workplaces. 25.____

A. Ephemeral B. Concrete C. Prosaic D. Aesthetic

KEY (CORRECT ANSWERS)

1. C
2. D
3. C
4. C
5. D

6. D
7. C
8. C
9. D
10. D

11. A
12. C
13. D
14. D
15. B

16. B
17. D
18. B
19. B
20. B

21. A
22. B
23. D
24. C
25. D

TEST 2

DIRECTIONS: Each question or incomplete statement is followed by several suggested answers or completions. Select the one that BEST answers the question or completes the statement. *PRINT THE LETTER OF THE CORRECT ANSWER IN THE SPACE AT THE RIGHT.*

1. In the communications process, a formal communication should contain a multiplicity of ideas and several related objectives in order to provide for time-saving economy and to enhance the prospects of eventual compliance by subordinates. 1.____
This statement is GENERALLY

   A. *true,* since it reduces to a minimum the need for issuance of frequent communications from policy-making levels
   B. *false,* since the number of ideas and objectives contained in a single communication operates in inverse ratio to the degree of compliance
   C. *true,* since continuity and cohesiveness of plans are developed by infrequent but elaborate formal communications
   D. *false,* since time-saving devices are not the concern of superiors engaged in developing an effective communications process

2. Experts in supervisory practices have been emphasizing the importance of the art of listening on the part of supervisors. A recently published text devotes over three hundred pages to a discussion on how managers and supervisors can improve their ability to listen. 2.____
Which one of the following is NOT considered an important rule to follow in developing the skill of listening?

   A. Be attentive and concentrate on what is being said.
   B. Concentrate on the spoken word without concern for implied meanings.
   C. Ask an occasional question when appropriate to the discussion.
   D. Make sure you understand fully what is being said.

3. A supervisor who is to direct a team of senior clerks and clerks in a complex project calls them together beforehand to inform them of the tasks each employee will perform on this job. 3.____
Of the following, the CHIEF value of this action by the supervisor is that each member of this team will be able to

   A. work independently in the absence of the supervisor
   B. understand what he will do and how this will fit into the total picture
   C. share in the process of decision-making as an equal participant
   D. judge how well the plans for this assignment have been made

4. A supervisor who has both younger and older employees under his supervision may sometimes find that employee absenteeism seriously interferes with accomplishment of goals. 4.____
Studies of such employee absenteeism have shown that the absences of employees

   A. under 35 years of age are usually unexpected and the absences of employees over 45 years are usually unnecessary
   B. of all age groups show the same characteristics as to length of absence

C. under 35 years of age are for frequent, short periods while the absences of employees over 45 years of age are less frequent but of longer duration
D. under 35 years of age are for periods of long duration and the absences of employees over 45 years of age are for periods of short duration

5. A long-standing procedure for getting a certain job done by subordinates is apparently a good procedure. Changes in some steps of the procedure are made from time to time to handle special problems that come up.
Reviewing this procedure periodically is *desirable* MAINLY because 5.____

A. the system is working well
B. checking routines periodically is a supervisor"s chief responsibility
C. subordinates may be confused as to how the procedure operates as a result of the changes made
D. it is necessary to determine whether the procedure has become outdated or is in need of improvement

6. In conducting an interview, the BEST type of questions with which to begin the interview are those which the person interviewed is ______ to answer. 6.____

A. willing and able
B. willing but unable
C. able to, but unwilling
D. unable and unwilling

7. In order to determine accurately a child's age, it is BEST for an interviewer to rely on 7.____

A. the child's grade in school
B. what the mother says
C. birth records
D. a library card

8. In his first interview with a new employee, it would be LEAST appropriate for a unit supervisor to 8.____

A. find out the employee's preference for the several types of jobs to which he is able to assign him
B. determine whether the employee will make good promotion material
C. inform the employee of what his basic job responsibilities will be
D. inquire about the employee's education and previous employment

9. If an interviewer takes care to phrase his questions carefully and precisely, the result will MOST probably be that 9.____

A. he will be able to determine whether the person interviewed is being truthful
B. the free flow of the interview will be lost
C. he will get the information he wants
D. he will ask stereotyped questions and narrow the scope of the interview

10. During an interview, the person interviewed is LEAST likely to be cautious about what he tells the interviewer 10.____

A. shortly after the beginning when the questions normally suggest pleasant associations to the person interviewed
B. as long as the interviewer keeps the questions to the point

C. at the point where the person interviewed gains a clear insight into the area being discussed
D. when the interview appears formally ended and good-byes are being said

11. In an interview held for the purpose of getting information from the person interviewed, it is sometimes desirable for the interviewer to repeat the answer he has received to a question. 11.____
For the interviewer to rephrase such an answer in his own words is good practice MAINLY because it

A. gives the interviewer time to make up his next question
B. gives the person interviewed a chance to correct any possible misunderstanding
C. gives the person interviewed the feeling that the interviewer considers his answer important
D. prevents the person interviewed from changing his answer

12. There are several methods of formulating questions during an interview. The particular method used should be adapted to the interview problems presented by the person being questioned. 12.____
Of the following methods of formulating questions during an interview, the ACCEPTABLE one is for the interviewer to ask questions which

A. incorporate several items in order to allow a cooperative interviewee freedom to organize his statements
B. are ambiguous in order to foil a distrustful inter-viewee
C. suggest the correct answer in order to assist an interviewee who appears confused
D. would help an otherwise unresponsive interviewee to become more responsive

13. An interviewer permits the person being interviewed to read the data the interviewer writes as he records the person's responses on a routine departmental form. This practice is 13.____

A. *desirable,* because it serves to assure the person interviewed that his responses are being recorded accurately
B. *undesirable,* because it prevents the interviewer from clarifying uncertain points by asking additional questions
C. *desirable,* because it makes the time that the person interviewed must wait while the answer is written seem shorter
D. *undesirable,* because it destroys the confidentiality of the interview

14. Suppose that a stranger enters the office of which you are in charge and asks for the address and telephone number of one of your employees. 14.____
The MOST appropriate reaction would be to

A. find out why he needs the information and release it if his reason is a good one
B. explain that you are not permitted to release such information to unauthorized persons
C. give him the information but tell him it must be kept confidential
D. ask him to leave the office immediately

15. A member of the public approaches an employee who is at work at his desk. The employee cannot interrupt his work in order to take care of this person. 15.____
The BEST and MOST courteous way of handling this situation is for the employee to

A. avoid looking up from his work until he is finished with what he is doing
B. tell this person that he will not be able to take care of him for quite a while
C. refer the individual to another employee who can take care of him right away
D. chat with the individual while he continues with his work

16. Some organizations, as a matter of policy, transfer their administrative staff personnel from one unit to another after stated periods of service in the unit. 16.____
The MAIN advantage of such a policy is that it

A. helps keep the staff members abreast of the technical developments in their fields
B. impedes the formation of personal cliques among staff members
C. helps develop wider outlook and loyalty to the organization as a whole rather than to the unit assigned
D. permits the more effective utilization of the individual talents of staff members

17. Leaders generally are somewhat more intelligent than their followers. 17.____
The CHIEF difficulty of the leader who is markedly more intelligent than his followers is that a leader has difficulty in

A. overcoming the suspicion and distrust of intellectuals on the part of the group
B. understanding the thought processes of persons who are intellectually inferior
C. accepting the irrational and emotional basis of much of human conduct
D. making himself understood by the group

18. A psychological study of leadership found that it is possible to predict the behavior of a new man in a leadership position more accurately on the basis of the behavior of his predecessor in the position than on the behavior of the man himself in his previous job. 18.____
The BEST explanation of this observation is that there is a tendency

A. to select similar types of personalities to fill the same type of position
B. for a newly appointed man to avoid instituting basic changes in operational procedures
C. for a given organizational structure and set of duties to produce similar patterns of behavior
D. for increased responsibility to impose more mature patterns of behavior on an incumbent

19. An administrative official finds that the reports reaching him from his subordinates tend to exaggerate the favorable and minimize the unfavorable aspects of situations existing within the unit. 19.____
The MOST valid conclusion to draw is that

A. the administrative official has been overly severe with subordinates and has instilled fear in them
B. there is a normal tendency for persons to represent themselves and their actions in the best possible light
C. members of the department tend to be optimists
D. the administrative official has not been sufficiently critical of previous reports and has not been alert to conditions in the unit

20. A special unit of a department is rife with rumors concerning plans for its future and the possibility of its abolition. As a result, morale and productivity of members assigned to it have suffered. To handle this situation, the administrative official in charge of the unit adopts a policy of promptly corroborating factual rumors and denying false ones. This method of dealing with the problem will achieve some good results, but its CHIEF weakness is that 20.____

A. it gives status to the rumors by the attention paid to them
B. the administrative official may not have the necessary information at hand to dispose promptly of all rumors
C. it *chases* the rumors rather than forestalling them by giving information concerning the unit's future
D. the administrative official may have confidential information which he should not divulge

21. An administrative official, realizing the importance of harmonious relationships within his unit, made a practice of unobtrusively intervening in any conflict situation between subordinates. Whenever friction seemed to be developing, he would attempt to soothe ruffled feelings, remove the source of difficulty by rescheduling activities or reassigning personnel,et cetera. His efforts were always behind-the-scenes and unknown to the employees involved. Although this method of operation produces some good results, its CHIEF drawback is that it 21.____

A. violates the chain of command principle
B. involves the administrative official in personal relationships which are not properly his concern
C. requires confidential sources of information about relationships within the unit, which borders on spying
D. permits subordinates to engage in unacceptable practices without correction

22. At a division conference at which a basic change in the department's procedure was to be announced, the conference leader started the discussion by asking the group for criticisms of the existing procedures. He then described the new procedures to be employed and explained the improvements in operations that were anticipated. The conference leader's method of introducing the change was 22.____

A. *good,* mainly because the conference members would be more receptive to the new procedure if they understood the inadequacies of the old
B. *bad,* mainly because the conference members would realize that the decision for change had been made before the discussion and without consideration of their comments
C. *good,* mainly because the comments and criticisms of the old procedure would provide the basis for evaluating the feasibility of the new method
D. *bad,* mainly because the focus of the discussion was on the procedure being replaced rather than on the procedure being introduced

23. A section chief in charge of a specialized unit calls a staff conference to discuss a proposed modification of some procedures. After making some introductory remarks, the chief wants the comments of the members of the staff. The staff consists of eight subordinates ranging in rank from office aide to principal administrative assistant III, each subordinate having responsibility for a different aspect of the program. Of the following, the BEST procedure for the chief to follow is to call upon each subordinate in 23.____

A. descending order of rank, mainly because the employees with the highest rank are likely to have the most experience and ability
B. ascending order of rank, mainly because the junior employees are more likely to be freer in their comments if they give their views before the senior employees speak
C. order of their specialized knowledge and competence in the subjects under discussion mainly because those with most knowledge and competence can best lead the discussion
D. order of seating around the table, mainly because informality of procedure and democrative leadership is obtained

24. As a supervisor assigned to a public relations unit in a city agency, you find a certain program under severe attack by a citizen's, group. 24.____
To be of GREATEST value to your supervisor, you should

A. present the department side of the story to all meetings or to all groups whether hostile or not
B. attempt to get another citizen's group to defend the department program
C. get greater support from the general public and the press to effectuate the program
D. ignore group opinions; rather, strive to affect individuals and let them persuade their groups

25. The commission has assigned you to present the department side to a group of citizens well-disposed to government programs. 25.____
You should present

A. *only* the department side
B. both sides of the story, but present the department side last
C. both sides of the story, but present the department side first
D. the facts and let the audience draw its own conclusion

KEY (CORRECT ANSWERS)

1. B
2. B
3. B
4. C
5. D
6. A
7. C
8. B
9. C
10. D
11. B
12. D
13. A
14. B
15. C
16. C
17. D
18. C
19. B
20. C
21. D
22. B
23. C
24. B
25. A

TEST 3

DIRECTIONS: Each question or incomplete statement is followed by several suggested answers or completions. Select the one that BEST answers the question or completes the statement. *PRINT THE LETTER OF THE CORRECT ANSWER IN THE SPACE AT THE RIGHT.*

1. Supervisor X, as a representative of the Commissioner, has been ordered to present the department arguments in reference to a new program of inspections and to emphasize such presentation by stressing the enforcement that will follow. 1.____
   In this instance,
   A. a mild threat is less of a deterrent than a strong threat
   B. any form of threat should be avoided since you are seeking cooperation
   C. an overly strong threat is less of a deterrent than a mild threat
   D. the mere statement that enforcement will follow is sufficient to effect cooperation

2. If, after an investigation and further consultation with central authorities, wholesale bribe-taking has been confirmed within a certain unit, the agency involved should 2.____
   A. withhold information from the public until a more secure image can be created
   B. break the story since such agency can present the least damaging picture
   C. arrange a compromise solution and present it to the public as an accomplished fact
   D. permit the central authorities to break the story since it presents a more efficient picture

3. The characteristic of flexibility versus stability of a policy seems contradictory to subordinate A. 3.____
   The difference can BEST be explained by the administrative manager if he points out that
   A. policies are decision guides and definite formulae for specific actions; therefore, stability must outweigh flexibility
   B. changing events and materials force a change in policy; therefore, flexibility refers to the ability to change policy when it becomes outmoded
   C. policy should be as stable as possible but sufficiently flexible to handle problems that vary from the normal; policy's true purpose must be understood as a guide for decisions, not an inflexible formula for action
   D. most policy at unit level is based on precedent and tradition and, therefore, subject always to the discretion of the supervisor

4. When an administrative manager devotes too much time to telling his subordinates how to handle their job problems, then he 4.____
   A. is spending too little time in formulating policies for the guidance of his subordinates
   B. is neglecting to delegate sufficient authority to his subordinates
   C. should immediately begin to plan for better use of his time
   D. should evaluate his approach to the administration of his section and establish better controls

5. Since the policies of a department are well established, an administrator does not need to formulate section policy. This statement is 5.____

   A. *true;* it is difficult for an administrator to establish a policy which will not in some way coincide or contradict established, overall policies
   B. *false;* department policies have to be broad enough to cover the whole organization; they are seldom detailed enough to guide a section in its internal organization
   C. *true;* the administrator's responsibility in this area is to formulate procedure to implement department policy
   D. *false;* uniformity of enforcement is essential, and this is impossible when the administrator does not establish his own section policy

6. Manager X, when giving a decision on a controversial item, reminds the subordinates of the policy under which such a decision was made. 6.____
This reminder is

   A. *good;* the subordinates will be aware that he is not being arbitrary, operating by whim, or playing favorites
   B. *unnecessary;* policies have been explained over and over again to subordinates
   C. a form of buck-passing since the manager is blaming a policy for his unfavorable decision
   D. *bad;* policy commits management to specific decisions and, as such, should not be given unfavorable publicity

7. After objectives and policies have been stated, the next step should be to 7.____

   A. develop plans and procedures
   B. make forecasts
   C. examine conditions; gather data
   D. consider a budget

8. After establishing objectives and identifying problems and opportunities, the planning should be 8.____

   A. turned over to the controller. You can alter his plan if you do not agree.
   B. assigned to the division heads. Each will work out a plan for his own division
   C. a joint effort of the controller and other division heads. You and any staff experts available will cooperate and assist as planning progresses.
   D. a joint effort of all supervisors and subordinates

9. The MOST; accurate statement concerning plans and planning is: 9.____

   A. In the absence of an agency-wide plan, it is better to avoid planning in the individual work unit
   B. Every manager or supervisor must plan if he is to carry out his managerial functions
   C. Every manager should make a preliminary plan and then await the agency-wide plan
   D. The agency-wide plan should precede the preliminary plan

10. Objectives, programs, policies, budgets, and procedures are all ______ planning. 10.____

   A. elements of overall
   B. guides for
   C. alternates to
   D. methods of

11. Developing and understanding objectives, establishing policies, collecting data, developing alternative action proposals, and deciding on action are all 11.____

A. steps in planning
B. guidelines to consider in planning
C. the action motif ascribed to planning
D. alternatives to planning

12. Work measurement can be applied to operations where workload can be related to 12.____

A. available personnel for the implementation of assigned tasks
B. follow-up programs for continued progress
C. cost abatement and optimum efficiency
D. man-hour utilization on assigned tasks

13. If you ask for additional historical information on costs, caseloads, et cetera, you will be 13.____

A. refining the forecast process
B. developing the groundwork for forecasting
C. estimating the future
D. evaluating your research department's efficiency

14. Suppose that the majority of mathematical projections predicts a serious downturn in new cases, while you and your advisors believe that a mild upturn is approaching. In this situation, the BEST procedure is to 14.____

A. follow the course dictated by the mathematical projections because that is what they are there for
B. follow your own ideas and those of your advisors; management is an art, not a science
C. modify the course dictated by the mathematical projections so as to reflect both management and specialist judgment
D. consult another advisor

15. The director of a personnel bureau with 100 employees would probably operate MOST efficiently if he had under his immediate supervision approximately ______ subordinates. 15.____

A. 5 B. 25 C. 50 D. 100

16. A worker is *usually* MOST productive when he is assigned to work which 16.____

A. he is able to do best
B. involves a variety of skills
C. is under close supervision
D. requires little skill

17. It is desirable for all staff specialists to have some knowledge of line activities PRIMARILY in order that they may 17.____

A. direct line activities when necessary
B. have a proper framework for research
C. know how to deal with all types of personnel
D. take cognizance of the agency's needs and problems

18. When a supervisor delegates an assignment, he should 18.____

A. delegate his responsibility for the assignment
B. make certain that the assignment is properly performed
C. participate in the beginning and final stages of the assignment
D. retain all authority needed to complete the assignment

19. Which one of the following is LEAST important in the management of a suggestion program? 19.____

A. Giving awards which are of sufficient value to encourage competition
B. Securing full support from the department's officers and executives
C. Publicizing the program and the awards given
D. Providing suggestion boxes in numerous locations

20. The MOST certain means to *decrease* morale is to 20.____

A. insist on strict adherence to safety rules
B. make each employee responsible for the tidiness of his work area
C. overlook evidence of hostility between groups of employees
D. provide strong, aggressive leadership

KEY (CORRECT ANSWERS)

1.	C	11.	A
2.	B	12.	D
3.	C	13.	B
4.	A	14.	C
5.	B	15.	A
6.	A	16.	A
7.	C	17.	D
8.	C	18.	B
9.	B	19.	D
10.	A	20.	C

READING COMPREHENSION
UNDERSTANDING AND INTERPRETING WRITTEN MATERIAL
EXAMINATION SECTION
TEST 1

DIRECTIONS: Each question or incomplete statement is followed by several suggested answers or completions. Select the one that BEST answers the question or completes the statement. *PRINT THE LETTER OF THE CORRECT ANSWER IN THE SPACE AT THE RIGHT.*

Questions 1-3.

DIRECTIONS: Questions 1 through 3 are to be answered SOLELY on the basis of the following statement.

The equipment in a mailroom may include a mail metering machine. This machine simultaneously stamps, postmarks, seals, and counts letters as fast as the operator can feed them. It can also print the proper postage directly on a gummed strip to be affixed to bulky items. It is equipped with a meter which is removed from the machine and sent to the postmaster to be set for a given number of stampings of any denomination. The setting of the meter must be paid for in advance. One of the advantages of metered mail is that it bypasses the cancellation operation and thereby facilitates handling by the post office. Mail metering also makes the pilfering of stamps impossible, but does not prevent the passage of personal mail in company envelopes through the meters unless there is established a rigid control or censorship over outgoing mail.

1. According to this statement, the postmaster 1.____
   A. is responsible for training new clerks in the use of mail metering machines
   B. usually recommends that both large and small firms adopt the use of mail metering machines
   C. is responsible for setting the meter to print a fixed number of stampings
   D. examines the mail metering machine to see that they are properly installed in the mailroom

2. According to this statement, the use of mail metering machines 2.____
   A. requires the employment of more clerks in a mailroom than does the use of postage stamps
   B. interferes with the handling of large quantities of outgoing mail
   C. does not prevent employees from sending their personal letters at company expense
   D. usually involves smaller expenditures for mailroom equipment than does the use of postage stamps

3. On the basis of this statement, it is MOST accurate to state that 3.____
   A. mail metering machines are often used for opening envelopes
   B. postage stamps are generally used when bulky packages are to be mailed
   C. the use of metered mail tends to interfere with rapid mail handling by the post office
   D. mail metering machines can seal and count letters at the same time

Questions 4-5.

DIRECTIONS: Questions 4 and 5 are to be answered SOLELY on the basis of the following statement.

Forms are printed sheets of paper on which information is to be entered. While what is printed on the form is most important, the kind of paper used in making the form is also important. The kind of paper should be selected with regard to the use to which the form will be subjected. Printing a form on an unnecessarily expensive grade of papers is wasteful. On the other hand, using too cheap or flimsy a form can materially interfere with satisfactory performance of the work the form is being planned to do. Thus, a form printed on both sides normally requires a heavier paper than a form printed only on one side. Forms to be used as permanent records, or which are expected to have a very long life in files, requires a quality of paper which will not disintegrate or discolor with age. A form which will go through a great deal of handling requires a strong, tough paper, while thinness is a necessary qualification where the making of several copies of a form will be required.

4. According to this statement, the type of paper used for making forms 4.____

   A. should be chosen in accordance with the use to which the form will be put
   B. should be chosen before the type of printing to be used has been decided upon
   C. is as important as the information which is printed on it
   D. should be strong enough to be used for any purpose

5. According to this statement, forms that are 5.____

   A. printed on both sides are usually economical and desirable
   B. to be filed permanently should not deteriorate as time goes on
   C. expected to last for a long time should be handled carefully
   D. to be filed should not be printed on inexpensive paper

Questions 6-8.

DIRECTIONS: Questions 6 through 8 are to be answered SOLELY on the basis of the following paragraph.

The increase in the number of public documents in the last two centuries closely matches the increase in population in the United States. The great number of public documents has become a serious threat to their usefulness. It is necessary to have programs which will reduce the number of public documents that are kept and which will, at the same time, assure keeping those that have value. Such programs need a great deal of thought to have any success.

6. According to the above paragraph, public documents may be LESS useful if 6.____

   A. the files are open to the public
   B. the record room is too small
   C. the copying machine is operated only during normal working hours
   D. too many records are being kept

7. According to the above paragraph, the growth of the population in the United States has matched the growth in the quantity of public documents for a period of MOST NEARLY _____ years. 7.____

A. 50 B. 100 C. 200 D. 300

8. According to the above paragraph, the increased number of public documents has made it necessary to 8.____

A. find out which public documents are worth keeping
B. reduce the great number of public documents by decreasing government services
C. eliminate the copying of all original public documents
D. avoid all new copying devices

Questions 9-10.

DIRECTIONS: Questions 9 and 10 are to be answered SOLELY on the basis of the following paragraph.

The work goals of an agency can best be reached if the employees understand and agree with these goals. One way to gain such understanding and agreement is for management to encourage and seriously consider suggestions from employees in the setting of agency goals.

9. On the basis of the above paragraph, the BEST way to achieve the work goals of an agency is to 9.____

A. make certain that employees work as hard as possible
B. study the organizational structure of the agency
C. encourage employees to think seriously about the agency's problems
D. stimulate employee understanding of the work goals

10. On the basis of the above paragraph, understanding and agreement with agency goals can be gained by 10.____

A. allowing the employees to set agency goals
B. reaching agency goals quickly
C. legislative review of agency operations
D. employee participation in setting agency goals

Questions 11-13.

DIRECTIONS: Questions 11 through 13 are to be answered SOLELY on the basis of the following paragraph.

In order to organize records properly, it is necessary to start from their very beginning and trace each copy of the record to find out how it is used, how long it is used, and what may finally be done with it. Although several copies of the record are made, one copy should be marked as the copy of record. This is the formal legal copy, held to meet the requirements of the law. The other copies may be retained for brief periods for reference purposes, but these copies should not be kept after their usefulness as reference ends. There is another reason for tracing records through the office and that is to determine how long it takes the copy of record to reach the central file. The copy of record must not be kept longer than necessary by the section of the office which has prepared it, but should be sent to the central file as soon as possible so that it can be available to the various sections of the office. The central file can make the copy of record available to the various sections of the office at an early date only if it arrives at the central file as quickly as possible. Just as soon as its immediate or active service period is ended, the copy of record should be removed from the central file and put into the inactive file in the office to be stored for whatever length of time may be necessary to meet legal requirements, and then destroyed.

11. According to the above paragraph, a reason for tracing records through an office is to 11.____

    A. determine how long the central file must keep the records
    B. organize records properly
    C. find out how many copies of each record are required
    D. identify the copy of record

12. According to the above paragraph, in order for the central file to have the copy of record available as soon as possible for the various sections of the office, it is MOST important that the 12.____

    A. copy of record to be sent to the central file meets the requirements of the law
    B. copy of record is not kept in the inactive file too long
    C. section preparing the copy of record does not unduly delay in sending it to the central file
    D. central file does not keep the copy of record beyond its active service period

13. According to the above paragraph, the length of time a copy of a record is kept in the inactive file of an office depends CHIEFLY on the 13.____

    A. requirements of the law
    B. length of time that is required to trace the copy of record through the office
    C. use that is made of the copy of record
    D. length of the period that the copy of record is used for reference purposes

Questions 14-16.

DIRECTIONS: Questions 14 through 16 are to be answered SOLELY on the basis of the following paragraph.

The office was once considered as nothing more than a focal point of internal and external correspondence. It was capable only of dispatching a few letters upon occasion and of preparing records of little practical value. Under such a concept, the vitality of the office force was impaired. Initiative became stagnant, and the lot of the office worker was not likely to be a happy one. However, under the new concept of office management, the possibilities of waste and mismanagement in office operation are now fully recognized, as are the possibilities for the modern office to assist in the direction and control of business operations. Fortunately, the modern concept of the office as a centralized service-rendering unit is gaining ever greater acceptance in today's complex business world, for without the modern office, the production wheels do not turn and the distribution of goods and services is not possible.

14. According to the above paragraph, the fundamental difference between the old and the new concept of the office is the change in the 14.____

 A. accepted functions of the office
 B. content and the value of the records kept
 C. office methods and systems
 D. vitality and morale of the office force

15. According to the above paragraph, an office operated today under the old concept of the office MOST likely would 15.____

 A. make older workers happy in their jobs
 B. be part of an old thriving business concern
 C. have a passive role in the conduct of a business enterprise
 D. attract workers who do not believe in modern methods

16. Of the following, the MOST important implication of the above paragraph is that a present-day business organization cannot function effectively without the 16.____

 A. use of modern office equipment
 B. participation and cooperation of the office
 C. continued modernization of office procedures
 D. employment of office workers with skill and initiative

Questions 17-20.

DIRECTIONS: Questions 17 through 20 are to be answered SOLELY on the basis of the following paragraph.

A report is frequently ineffective because the person writing it is not fully acquainted with all the necessary details before he actually starts to construct the report. All details pertaining to the subject should be known before the report is started. If the essential facts are not known, they should be investigated. It is wise to have essential facts written down rather than to depend too much on memory, especially if the facts pertain to such matters as amounts, dates, names of persons, or other specific data. When the necessary information has been gathered, the general plan and content of the report should be thought out before the writing is actually begun. A person with little or no experience in writing reports may find that it is wise to make a brief outline. Persons with more experience should not need a written outline, but they should make mental notes of the steps they are to follow. If writing reports without dictation is a regular part of an office worker's duties, he should set aside a certain time during the day when he is least likely to be interrupted. That may be difficult, but in most offices there are certain times in the day when the callers, telephone calls, and other interruptions are not numerous. During those times, it is best to write reports that need undivided concentration. Reports that are written amid a series of interruptions may be poorly done.

17. Before starting to write an effective report, it is necessary to 17.____

 A. memorize all specific information
 B. disregard ambiguous data
 C. know all pertinent information
 D. develop a general plan

18. Reports dealing with complex and difficult material should be 18.____

    A. prepared and written by the supervisor of the unit
    B. written when there is the least chance of interruption
    C. prepared and written as part of regular office routine
    D. outlined and then dictated

19. According to the paragraph, employees with no prior familiarity in writing reports may find it helpful to 19.____

    A. prepare a brief outline
    B. mentally prepare a synopsis of the report's content
    C. have a fellow employee help in writing the report
    D. consult previous reports

20. In writing a report, needed information which is unclear should be 20.____

    A. disregarded
    B. memorized
    C. investigated
    D. gathered

Questions 21-25.

DIRECTIONS: Questions 21 through 25 are to be answered SOLELY on the basis of the following passage.

Positive discipline minimizes the amount of personal supervision required and aids in the maintenance of standards. When a new employee has been properly introduced and carefully instructed, when he has come to know the supervisor and has confidence in the supervisor's ability to take care of him, when he willingly cooperates with the supervisor, that employee has been under positive discipline and can be put on his own to produce the quantity and quality of work desired. Negative discipline, the fear of transfer to a less desirable location, for example, to a limited extent may restrain certain individuals from overt violation of rules and regulations governing attendance and conduct which in governmental agencies are usually on at least an agency-wide basis. Negative discipline may prompt employees to perform according to certain rules to avoid a penalty such as, for example, docking for tardiness.

21. According to the above passage, it is reasonable to assume that in the area of discipline, the first-line supervisor in a governmental agency has GREATER scope for action in 21.____

    A. *positive* discipline, because negative discipline is largely taken care of by agency rules and regulations
    B. *negative* discipline, because rules and procedures are already fixed and the supervisor can rely on them
    C. *positive* discipline, because the supervisor is in a position to recommend transfers
    D. *negative* discipline, because positive discipline is reserved for people on a higher supervisory level

22. In order to maintain positive discipline of employees under his supervision, it is MOST important for a supervisor to 22.____

    A. assure each employee that he has nothing to worry about
    B. insist at the outset on complete cooperation from employees

C. be sure that each employee is well trained in his job
D. inform new employees of the penalties for not meeting standards

23. According to the above passage, a feature of negative discipline is that it 23.____

A. may lower employee morale
B. may restrain employees from disobeying the rules
C. censures equal treatment of employees
D. tends to create standards for quality of work

24. A REASONABLE conclusion based on the above passage is that positive discipline benefits a supervisor because 24.____

A. he can turn over orientation and supervision of a new employee to one of his subordinates
B. subordinates learn to cooperate with one another when working on an assignment
C. it is easier to administer
D. it cuts down, in the long run, on the amount of time the supervisor needs to spend on direct supervision

25. Based on the above passage, it is REASONABLE to assume, that an important difference between positive discipline and negative discipline is that positive discipline 25.____

A. is concerned with the quality of work and negative discipline with the quantity of work
B. leads to a more desirable basis for motivation of the employee
C. is more likely to be concerned with agency rules and regulations
D. uses fear while negative discipline uses penalties to prod employees to adequate performance

KEY (CORRECT ANSWERS)

1. C
2. C
3. D
4. A
5. B
6. D
7. C
8. A
9. D
10. D
11. B
12. C
13. A
14. A
15. C
16. B
17. C
18. B
19. A
20. B
21. A
22. C
23. B
24. D
25. B

TEST 2

Questions 1-6.

DIRECTIONS: Questions 1 through 6 are to be answered SOLELY on the basis of the following passage.

Inherent in all organized endeavors is the need to resolve the individual differences involved in conflict. Conflict may be either a positive or negative factor since it may lead to creativity, innovation and progress on the one hand, or it may result, on the other hand, in a deterioration or even destruction of the organization. Thus, some forms of conflict are desirable, whereas others are undesirable and ethically wrong.

There are three management strategies which deal with interpersonal conflict. In the *divide-and-rule strategy,* management attempts to maintain control by limiting the conflict to those directly involved and preventing their disagreement from spreading to the larger group. The *suppression-of-differences strategy* entails ignoring conflicts or pretending they are irrelevant. In the *working-through-differences strategy,* management actively attempts to solve or resolve intergroup or interpersonal conflicts. Of the three strategies, only the last directly attacks and has the potential for eliminating the causes of conflict. An essential part of this strategy, however, is its employment by a committed and relatively mature management team.

1. According to the above passage, the *divide-and-rule strategy tor* dealing with conflict is the attempt to 1.____

   A. involve other people in the conflict
   B. restrict the conflict to those participating in it
   C. divide the conflict into positive and negative factors
   D. divide the conflict into a number of smaller ones

2. The word *conflict* is used in relation to both positive and negative factors in this passage. Which one of the following words is MOST likely to describe the activity which the word *conflict,* in the sense of the passage, implies? 2.____

   A. Competition
   B. Confusion
   C. Cooperation
   D. Aggression

3. According to the above passage, which one of the following characteristics is shared by both the *suppression-of-differences strategy* and the *divide-and-rule strategy*? 3.____

   A. Pretending that conflicts are irrelevant
   B. Preventing conflicts from spreading to the group situation
   C. Failure to directly attack the causes of conflict
   D. Actively attempting to resolve interpersonal conflict

4. According to the above passage, the successful resolution of interpersonal conflict requires 4.____

   A. allowing the group to mediate conflicts between two individuals
   B. division of the conflict into positive and negative factors
   C. involvement of a committed, mature management team
   D. ignoring minor conflicts until they threaten the organization

5. Which can be MOST reasonably inferred from the above passage? Conflict between two individuals is LEAST likely to continue when management uses 5.____

   A. the *working-through differences strategy*
   B. the *suppression-of differences strategy*
   C. the *divide-and-rule strategy*
   D. a combination of all three strategies

6. According to the above passage, a DESIRABLE result of conflict in an organization is when conflict 6.____

   A. exposes production problems in the organization
   B. can be easily ignored by management
   C. results in advancement of more efficient managers
   D. leads to development of new methods

Questions 7-13.

DIRECTIONS: Questions 7 through 13 are to be answered SOLELY on the basis of the passage below.

Modern management places great emphasis on the concept of communication. The communication process consists of the steps through which an idea or concept passes from its inception by one person, the sender, until it is acted upon by another person, the receiver. Through an understanding of these steps and some of the possible barriers that may occur, more effective communication may be achieved. The first step in the communication process is ideation by the sender. This is the formation of the intended content of the message he wants to transmit. In the next step, encoding, the sender organizes his ideas into a series of symbols designed to communicate his message to his intended receiver. He selects suitable words or phrases that can be understood by the receiver, and he also selects the appropriate media to be used—for example, memorandum, conference, etc. The third step is transmission of the encoded message through selected channels in the organizational structure. In the fourth step, the receiver enters the process by tuning in to receive the message. If the receiver does not function, however, the message is lost. For example, if the message is oral, the receiver must be a good listener. The fifth step is decoding of the message by the receiver, as for example, by changing words into ideas. At this step, the decoded message may not be the same idea that the sender originally encoded because the sender and receiver have different perceptions regarding the meaning of certain words. Finally, the receiver acts or responds. He may file the information, ask for more information, or take other action. There can be no assurance, however, that communication has taken place unless there is some type of feedback to the sender in the form of an acknowledgement that the message was received.

7. According to the above passage, *ideation* is the process by which the 7.____

   A. sender develops the intended content of the message
   B. sender organizes his ideas into a series of symbols
   C. receiver tunes in to receive the message
   D. receiver decodes the message

8. In the last sentence of the passage, the word *feedback* refers to the process by which the sender is assured that the 8.____

   A. receiver filed the information
   B. receiver's perception is the same as his own
   C. message was received
   D. message was properly interpreted

9. Which one of the following BEST shows the order of the steps in the communication process as described in the passage? 9.____

   A. 1 - ideation 2 - encoding
      3 - decoding 4 - transmission
      5 - receiving 6 - action
      7 - feedback to the sender

   B. 1 - ideation 2 - encoding
      3 - transmission 4 - decoding
      5 - receiving 6 - action
      7 - feedback to the sender

   C. 1 - ideation 2 - decoding
      3 - transmission 4 - receiving
      5 - encoding 6 - action
      7 - feedback to the sender

   D. 1 - ideation 2 - encoding
      3 - transmission 4 - receiving
      5 - decoding 6 - action
      7 - feedback to the sender

10. Which one of the following BEST expresses the main theme of the passage? 10.____

   A. Different individuals have the same perceptions regarding the meaning of words.
   B. An understanding of the steps in the communication process may achieve better communication.
   C. Receivers play a passive role in the communication process.
   D. Senders should not communicate with receivers who transmit feedback.

11. The above passage implies that a receiver does NOT function properly when he 11.____

   A. transmits feedback
   B. files the information
   C. is a poor listener
   D. asks for more information

12. Which one of the following, according to the above passage, is included in the SECOND step of the communication process? 12.____

   A. Selecting the appropriate media to be used in transmission
   B. Formulation of the intended content of the message
   C. Using appropriate media to respond to the receiver's feedback
   D. Transmitting the message through selected channels in the organization

13. The above passage implies that the *decoding process* is MOST NEARLY the reverse of the ______ process. 13.____

   A. transmission
   B. receiving
   C. feedback
   D. encoding

Questions 14-19.

DIRECTIONS: Questions 14 through 19 are to be answered SOLELY on the basis of the following passage.

It is often said that no system will work if the people who carry it out do not want it to work. In too many cases, a departmental reorganization that seemed technically sound and economically practical has proved to be a failure because the planners neglected to take the human factor into account. The truth is that employees are likely to feel threatened when they learn that a major change is in the wind. It does not matter whether or not the change actually poses a threat to an employee; the fact that he believes it does or fears it might is enough to make him feel insecure. Among the dangers he fears, the foremost is the possibility that his job may cease to exist and that he may be laid off or shunted into a less skilled position at lower pay. Even if he knows that his own job category is secure, however, he is likely to fear losing some of the important intangible advantages of his present position–for instance, he may fear that he will be separated from his present companions and thrust in with a group of strangers, or that he will find himself in a lower position on the organizational ladder if a new position is created above his.

It is important that management recognize these natural fears and take them into account in planning any kind of major change. While there is no cut-and-dried formula for preventing employee resistance, there are several steps that can be taken to reduce employees' fears and gain their cooperation. First, unwarranted fears can be dispelled if employees are kept informed of the planning from the start and if they know exactly what to expect. Next, assurance on matters such as retraining, transfers, and placement help should be given as soon as it is clear what direction the reorganization will take. Finally, employees' participation in the planning should be actively sought. There is a great psychological difference between feeling that a change is being forced upon one from the outside, and feeling that one is an insider who is helping to bring about a change.

14. According to the above passage, employees who are not in real danger of losing their jobs because of a proposed reorganization 14.____

    A. will be eager to assist in the reorganization
    B. will pay little attention to the reorganization
    C. should not be taken into account in planning the reorganization
    D. are nonetheless likely to feel threatened by the reorganization

15. The passage mentions the *intangible advantages* of a position. 15.____
    Which of the following BEST describes the kind of advantages alluded to in the passage?

    A. Benefits such as paid holidays and vacations
    B. Satisfaction of human needs for things like friendship and status
    C. Qualities such as leadership and responsibility
    D. A work environment that meets satisfactory standards of health and safety

16. According to the passage, an employee's fear that a reorganization may separate him from his present companions is a (n) 16.____

    A. childish and immature reaction to change
    B. unrealistic feeling since this is not going to happen

C. possible reaction that the planners should be aware of
D. incentive to employees to participate in the planning

17. On the basis of the above passage, it would be DESIRABLE, when planning a departmental reorganization, to 17.____

A. be governed by employee feelings and attitudes
B. give some employees lower positions
C. keep employees informed
D. lay off those who are less skilled

18. What does the passage say can be done to help gain employees' cooperation in a reorganization? 18.____

A. Making sure that the change is technically sound, that it is economically practical, and that the human factor is taken into account
B. Keeping employees fully informed, offering help in fitting them into new positions, and seeking their participation in the planning
C. Assuring employees that they will not be laid off, that they will not be reassigned to a group of strangers, and that no new positions will be created on the organization ladder
D. Reducing employees' fears, arranging a retraining program, and providing for transfers

19. Which of the following suggested titles would be MOST appropriate for this passage? 19.____

A. PLANNING A DEPARTMENTAL REORGANIZATION
B. WHY EMPLOYEES ARE AFRAID
C. LOOKING AHEAD TO THE FUTURE
D. PLANNING FOR CHANGE: THE HUMAN FACTOR

Questions 20-22.

DIRECTIONS: Questions 20 through 22 are to be answered SOLELY on the basis of the following passage.

The achievement of good human relations is essential if a business office is to produce at top efficiency and is to be a pleasant place in which to work. All office workers plan an important role in handling problems in human relations. They should, therefore, strive to acquire the understanding, tactfulness, and awareness necessary to deal effectively with actual office situations involving co-workers on all levels. Only in this way can they truly become responsible, interested, cooperative, and helpful members of the staff.

20. The selection implies that the MOST important value of good human relations in an office is to develop 20.____

A. efficiency
B. cooperativeness
C. tact
D. pleasantness and efficiency

21. Office workers should acquire understanding in dealing with 21.____

A. co-workers
B. subordinates
C. superiors
D. all members of the staff

22. The selection indicates that a highly competent secretary who is also very argumentative is meeting office requirements 22.____

A. wholly
B. partly
C. slightly
D. not at all

Questions 23-25.

DIRECTIONS: Questions 23 through 25 are to be answered SOLELY on the basis of the following passage.

It is common knowledge that ability to do a particular job and performance on the job do not always go hand in hand. Persons with great potential abilities sometimes fall down on the job because of laziness or lack of interest in the job, while persons with mediocre talents have often achieved excellent results through their industry and their loyalty to the interests of their employers. It is clear; therefore, that in a balanced personnel program, measures of employee ability need to be supplemented by measures of employee performance, for the final test of any employee is his performance on the job.

23. The MOST accurate of the following statements, on the basis of the above paragraph, is that 23.____

A. employees who lack ability are usually not industrious
B. an employee's attitudes are more important than his abilities
C. mediocre employees who are interested in their work are preferable to employees who possess great ability
D. superior capacity for performance should be supplemented with proper attitudes

24. On the basis of the above paragraph, the employee of most value to his employer is NOT necessarily the one who 24.____

A. best understands the significance of his duties
B. achieves excellent results
C. possesses the greatest talents
D. produces the greatest amount of work

25. According to the above paragraph, an employee's efficiency is BEST determined by an 25.____

A. appraisal of his interest in his work
B. evaluation of the work performed by him
C. appraisal of his loyalty to his employer
D. evaluation of his potential ability to perform his work

KEY (CORRECT ANSWERS)

1. B
2. A
3. C
4. C
5. A
6. D
7. A
8. C
9. D
10. B
11. C
12. A
13. D
14. D
15. B
16. C
17. C
18. B
19. D
20. D
21. D
22. B
23. D
24. C
25. B

TEST 3

Questions 1-8.

DIRECTIONS: Questions 1 through 8 are to be answered SOLELY on the basis of the following information and directions.

Assume that you are a clerk in a city agency. Your supervisor has asked you to classify each of the accidents that happened to employees in the agency into the following five categories:

A. An accident that occurred in the period from January through June, between 9 A.M. and 12 Noon, that was the result of carelessness on the part of the injured employee, that caused the employee to lose less than seven working hours, that happened to an employee who was 40 years of age or over, and who was employed in the agency for less than three years;

B. An accident that occurred in the period from July through December, after 1 P.M., that was the result of unsafe conditions, that caused the injured employee to lose less than seven working hours, that happened to an employee who was 40 years of age or over, and who was employed in the agency for three years or more;

C. An accident that occurred in the period from January through June, after 1 P.M., that was the result of carelessness on the part of the injured employee, that caused the injured employee to lose seven or more working hours, that happened to an employee who was less than 40 years old, and who was employed in the agency for three years or more;

D. An accident that occurred in the period from July through December, between 9 A.M. and 12 Noon, that was the result of unsafe conditions, that caused the injured employee to lose seven or more working hours, that happened to an employee who was less than 40 years old, and who was employed in the agency for less than three years;

E. Accidents that cannot be classified in any of the foregoing groups. NOTE: In classifying these accidents, an employee's age and length of service are computed as of the date of accident. In all cases, it is to be assumed that each employee has been employed continuously in city service, and that each employee works seven hours a day, from 9 A.M. to 5 P.M., with lunch from 12 Noon to 1 P.M. In each question, consider only the information which will assist you in classifying the accident. Any information which is of no assistance in classifying an accident should not be considered.

1. The unsafe condition of the stairs in the building caused Miss Perkins to have an accident on October 14, 2003 at 4 P.M. When she returned to work the following day at 1 P.M., Miss Perkins said that the accident was the first one that had occurred to her in her ten years of employment with the agency. She was born on April 27, 1962. 1.____

2. On the day after she completed her six-month probationary period of employment with the agency, Miss Green, who had been considered a careful worker by her supervisor, injured her left foot in an accident caused by her own carelessness. She went home immediately after the accident, which occurred at 10 A.M., March 19, 2004, but returned to work at the regular time on the following morning. Miss Green was born July 12, 1963 in New York City. 2.____

3. The unsafe condition of a duplicating machine caused Mr. Martin to injure himself in an accident on September 8, 2006 at 2 P.M. As a result of the accident, he was unable to work the remainder of the day, but returned to his office ready for work on the following morning. Mr. Martin, who has been working for the agency since April 1, 2003, was born in St. Louis on February 1, 1968. 3.____

4. Mr. Smith was hospitalized for two weeks because of a back injury resulted from an accident on the morning of November 16, 2006. Investigation of the accident revealed that it was caused by the unsafe condition of the floor on which Mr. Smith had been walking. Mr. Smith, who is an accountant, has been anemployee of the agency since March 1, 2004, and was born in Ohio on June 10, 1968. 4.____

5. Mr. Allen cut his right hand because he was careless in operating a multilith machine. Mr. Allen, who was 33 years old when the accident took place, has been employed by the agency since August 17, 1992. The accident, which occurred on January 26, 2006, at 2 P.M., caused Mr. Allen to be absent from work for the rest of the day. He was able to return to work the next morning. 5.____

6. Mr. Rand, who is a college graduate, was born on December, 28, 1967, and has been working for the agency since January 7, 2002. On Monday, April 25, 2005, at 2 P.M., his carelessness in operating a duplicating machine caused him to have an accident and to be sent home from work immediately. Fortunately, he was able to return to work at his regular time on the following Wednesday. 6.____

7. Because he was careless in running down a flight of stairs, Mr. Brown fell, bruising his right hand. Although the accident occurred shortly after he arrived for work on the morning of May 22, 2006, he was unable to resume work until 3 P.M. that day. Mr. Brown was born on August 15, 1955, and began working for the agency on September 12, 2003, as a clerk, at a salary of $22,750 per annum. 7.____

8. On December 5, 2005, four weeks after he had begun working for the agency, the unsafe condition of an automatic stapling machine caused Mr. Thomas to injure himself in an accident. Mr. Thomas, who was born on May 19,1975, lost three working days because of the accident, which occurred at 11:45 A.M. 8.____

Questions 9-10.

DIRECTIONS: Questions 9 and 10 are to be answered SOLELY on the basis of the following paragraph.

An impending reorganization within an agency will mean loss by transfer of several professional staff members from the personnel division. The division chief is asked to designate the persons to be transferred. After reviewing the implications of this reduction of staff with his assistant, the division chief discusses the matter at a staff meeting. He adopts the recommendations of several staff members to have volunteers make up the required reduction.

9. The decision to permit personnel to volunteer for transfer is 9.____

   A. *poor;* it is not likely that the members of a division are of equal value to the division chief
   B. *good;* dissatisfied members will probably be more productive elsewhere
   C. *poor;* the division chief has abdicated his responsibility to carry out the order given to him
   D. *good;* morale among remaining staff is likely to improve in a more cohesive framework

10. Suppose that one of the volunteers is a recently appointed employee who has completed his probationary period acceptably, but whose attitude toward division operations and agency administration tends to be rather negative and sometimes even abrasive. Because of his lack of commitment to the division, his transfer is recommended. If the transfer is approved, the division chief should, prior to the transfer, 10.____

   A. discuss with the staff the importance of commitment to the work of the agency and its relationship with job satisfaction
   B. refrain from any discussion of attitude with the employee
   C. discuss with the employee his concern about the employee's attitude
   D. avoid mention of attitude in the evaluation appraisal prepared for the receiving division chief

Questions 11-16.

DIRECTIONS: Questions 11 through 16 are to be answered SOLELY on the basis of the following paragraph.

Methods of administration of office activities, much of which consists of providing information and *know-how* needed to coordinate both activities within that particular office and other offices, have been among the last to come under the spotlight of management analysis. Progress has been rapid during the past decade, however, and is now accelerating at such a pace that an *information revolution* in office management appears to be in the making. Although triggered by technological breakthroughs in electronic computers and other giant steps in mechanization, this information revolution must be attributed to underlying forces, such as the increased complexity of both governmental and private enterprise, and ever-keener competition. Size, diversification, specialization of function, and decentralization are among the forces which make coordination of activities both more imperative and more difficult. Increased competition, both domestic and international, leaves little margin for error in managerial decisions. Several developments during recent years indicate an evolving pattern. In 1960, the American Management Association expanded the scope of its activities and changed the name of its Office Management Division to Administrative Services Division. Also in 1960, the magazine *Office Management* merged with the magazine *American Business,* and this new publication was named *Administrative Management.*

11. A REASONABLE inference that can be made from the information in the above paragraph is that an important role of the office manager today is to 11.____

A. work toward specialization of functions performed by his subordinates
B. inform and train subordinates regarding any new developments in computer technology and mechanization
C. assist the professional management analysts with the management analysis work in the organization
D. supply information that can be used to help coordinate and manage the other activities of the organization

12. An IMPORTANT reason for the *information revolution* that has been taking place in office management is the 12.____

A. advance made in management analysis in the past decade
B. technological breakthrough in electronic computers and mechanization
C. more competitive and complicated nature of private business and government
D. increased efficiency of office management techniques in the past ten years

13. According to the above paragraph, specialization of function in an organization is MOST likely to result in 13.____

A. the elimination of errors in managerial decisions
B. greater need to coordinate activities
C. more competition with other organizations, both domestic and international
D. a need for office managers with greater flexibility

14. The word *evolving,* as used in the third from last sentence in the above paragraph, means MOST NEARLY 14.____

A. developing by gradual changes
B. passing on to others
C. occurring periodically
D. breaking up into separate, constituent parts

15. Of the following, the MOST reasonable implication of the changes in names mentioned in the last part of the above paragraph is that these groups are attempting to 15.____

A. professionalize the field of office management and the title of Office Manager
B. combine two publications into one because of the increased costs of labor and materials
C. adjust to the fact that the field of office management is broadening
D. appeal to the top managerial people rather than the office management people in business and government

16. According to the above paragraph, intense competition among domestic and international enterprises makes it MOST important for an organization's managerial staff to 16.____

A. coordinate and administer office activities with other activities in the organization
B. make as few errors in decision-making as possible
C. concentrate on decentralization and reduction of size of the individual divisions of the organization
D. restrict decision-making only to top management officials

Questions 17-21.

DIRECTIONS: Questions 17 through 21 are to be answered SOLELY on the basis of the following passage.

For some office workers, it is useful to be familiar with the four main classes of domestic mail; for others, it is essential. Each class has a different rate of postage, and some have requirements concerning wrapping, sealing, or special information to be placed on the package. First class mail, the class which may not be opened for postal inspection, includes letters, postcards, business reply cards, and other kinds of written matter. There are different rates for some of the kinds of cards which can be sent by first class mail. The maximum weight for an item sent by first class mail is 70 pounds. An item which is not letter size should be marked *First Class* on all sides. Although office workers most often come into contact with first class mail, they may find it helpful to know something about the other classes. Second class mail is generally used for mailing newspapers and magazines. Publishers of these articles must meet certain U.S. Postal Service requirements in order to obtain a permit to use second class mailing rates. Third class mail, which must weigh less than 1 pound, includes printed materials and merchandise parcels. There are two rate structures for this class - a single piece rate and a bulk rate. Fourth class mail, also known as parcel post, includes packages weighing from one to 40 pounds. For more information about these classes of mail and the actual mailing rates, contact your local post office.

17. According to this passage, first class mail is the *only* class which 17.____

A. has a limit on the maximum weight of an item
B. has different rates for items within the class
C. may not be opened for postal inspection
D. should be used by office workers

18. According to this passage, the one of the following items which may CORRECTLY be sent by fourth class mail is a 18.____

A. magazine weighing one-half pound
B. package weighing one-half pound
C. package weighing two pounds
D. postcard

19. According to this passage, there are different postage rates for 19.____

A. a newspaper sent by second class mail and a magazine sent by second class mail
B. each of the classes of mail
C. each pound of fourth class mail
D. printed material sent by third class mail and merchandise parcels sent by third class mail

20. In order to send a newspaper by second class mail, a publisher MUST 20.____

A. have met certain postal requirements and obtained a permit
B. indicate whether he wants to use the single piece or the bulk rate
C. make certain that the newspaper weighs less than one pound
D. mark the newspaper *Second Class* on the top and bottom of the wrapper

21. Of the following types of information, the one which is NOT mentioned in the passage is the 21.____

    A. class of mail to which parcel post belongs
    B. kinds of items which can be sent by each class of mail
    C. maximum weight for an item sent by fourth class mail
    D. postage rate for each of the four classes of mail

Questions 22-25.

DIRECTIONS: Questions 22 through 25 are to be answered SOLELY on the basis of the following paragraph.

A standard comprises characteristics attached to an aspect of a process or product by which it can be evaluated. Standardization is the development and adoption of standards. When they are formulated, standards are not usually the product of a single person, but represent the thoughts and ideas of a group, leavened with the knowledge and information which are currently available. Standards which do not meet certain basic requirements become a hindrance rather than an aid to progress. Standards must not only be correct, accurate, and precise in requiring no more and no less than what is needed for satisfactory results, but they must also be workable in the sense that their usefulness is not nullified by external conditions. Standards should also be acceptable to the people who use them. If they are not acceptable, they cannot be considered to be satisfactory, although they may possess all the other essential characteristics.

22. According to the above paragraph, a processing standard that requires the use of materials that cannot be procured is MOST likely to be 22.____

    A. incomplete
    B. unworkable
    C. inaccurate
    D. unacceptable

23. According to the above paragraph, the construction of standards to which the performance of job duties should conform is MOST often 23.____

    A. the work of the people responsible for seeing that the duties are properly performed
    B. accomplished by the person who is best informed about the functions involved
    C. the responsibility of the people who are to apply them
    D. attributable to the efforts of various informed persons

24. According to the above paragraph, when standards call for finer tolerances than those essential to the conduct of successful production operations, the effect of the standards on the improvement of production operations is 24.____

    A. negative
    B. negligible
    C. nullified
    D. beneficial

25. The one of the following which is the MOST suitable title for the above paragraph is 25.____

    A. THE EVALUATION OF FORMULATED STANDARDS
    B. THE ATTRIBUTES OF SATISFACTORY STANDARDS
    C. THE ADOPTION OF ACCEPTABLE STANDARDS
    D. THE USE OF PROCESS OR PRODUCT STANDARDS

KEY (CORRECT ANSWERS)

1. B
2. A
3. E
4. D
5. E
6. C
7. A
8. D
9. A
10. C
11. D
12. C
13. B
14. A
15. C
16. B
17. C
18. C
19. B
20. A
21. D
22. C
23. D
24. A
25. B

PREPARING WRITTEN MATERIAL

PARAGRAPH REARRANGEMENT COMMENTARY

The sentences that follow are in scrambled order. You are to rearrange them in proper order and indicate the letter choice containing the correct answer at the space at the right.

Each group of sentences in this section is actually a paragraph presented in scrambled order. Each sentence in the group has a place in that paragraph; no sentence is to be left out. You are to read each group of sentences and decide upon the best order in which to put the sentences so as to form a well-organized paragraph.

The questions in this section measure the ability to solve a problem when all the facts relevant to its solution are not given.

More specifically, certain positions of responsibility and authority require the employee to discover connection between events sometimes, apparently, unrelated. In order to do this, the employee will find it necessary to correctly infer that unspecified events have probably occurred or are likely to occur. This ability becomes especially important when action must be taken on incomplete information.

Accordingly, these questions require competitors to choose among several suggested alternatives, each of which presents a different sequential arrangement of the events. Competitors must choose the MOST logical of the suggested sequences.

In order to do so, they may be required to draw on general knowledge to infer missing concepts or events that are essential to sequencing the given events. Competitors should be careful to infer only what is essential to the sequence. The plausibility of the wrong alternatives will always require the inclusion of unlikely events or of additional chains of events which are NOT essential to sequencing the given events.

It's very important to remember that you are looking for the best of the four possible choices, and that the best choice of all may not even be one of the answers you're given to choose from.

There is no one right way to solve these problems. Many people have found it helpful to first write out the order of the sentences, as they would have arranged them, on their scrap paper before looking at the possible answers. If their optimum answer is there, this can save them some time. If it isn't, this method can still give insight into solving the problem. Others find it most helpful to just go through each of the possible choices, contrasting each as they go along. You should use whatever method feels comfortable and works for you.

While most of these types of questions are not that difficult, we've added a higher percentage of the difficult type, just to give you more practice. Usually there are only one or two questions on this section that contain such subtle distinctions that you're unable to answer confidently. And you then may find yourself stuck deciding between two possible choices, neither of which you're sure about.

EXAMINATION SECTION

TEST 1

DIRECTIONS: The sentences that follow are in scrambled order. You are to rearrange them in proper order and indicate the letter choice containing the correct answer. *PRINT THE LETTER OF THE CORRECT ANSWER IN THE SPACE AT THE RIGHT.*

1. Below are four statements labeled W, X, Y and Z. 1.____
   W. He was a strict and fanatic drillmaster.
   X. The word is always used in a derogatory sense and generally shows resentment and anger on the part of the user.
   Y. It is from the name of this Frenchman that we derive our English word, martinet.
   Z. Jean Martinet was the Inspector-General of Infantry during the reign of King Louis XIV.

   The PROPER order in which these sentences should be placed in a paragraph is:
   A. X, Z, W, Y B. X, Z, Y, W C. Z, W, Y, X D. Z, Y, W, X

2. In the following paragraph, the sentences, which are numbered, have been jumbled. 2.____
   I. Since then it has undergone changes.
   II. It was incorporated in 1955 under the laws of the State of New York.
   III. Its primary purposes, a cleaner city, has, however, remained the same.
   IV. The Citizens Committee works in cooperation with the Mayor's Inter-departmental Committee for a Clean City. 3.____

   The order in which these sentences should be arranged to form a well-organized paragraph is:
   A. II, IV, I, III B. III, IV, I, II C. IV, II, I, III D. IV, III, II, I

Questions 3-5.

DIRECTIONS: The sentences listed below are part of a meaningful paragraph but they are not given in their proper order. You are to decide what would be the BEST order in which to put the sentences so as to form a well-organized paragraph. Each sentence has a place in the paragraph; there are no extra sentences. You are then to answer Questions 3 through 5 inclusive on the basis of your rearrangements of these scrambled sentences into a properly organized paragraph.

In 1887 some insurance companies organized an Inspection Department to advise their clients on all phases of fire prevention and protection. Probably this has been due to the smaller annual fire losses in Great Britain than in the United States. It tests various fire prevention devices and appliances and determines manufacturing hazards and their safeguards. Fire research began earlier in the United States and is more advanced than in Great Britain. Later they established a laboratory specializing in electrical, mechanical, hydraulic, and chemical fields.

3. When the five sentences are arranged in proper order, the paragraph starts with the sentence which begins 3.____
   A. "In 1887..." B. "Probably this..." C. "It tests..."
   D. "Fire research..." E. "Later they..."

4. In the last sentence listed above, "they" refers to 4.____
   A. the insurance companies B. the United States and Great Britain
   C. the Inspection Department D. clients
   E. technicians

5. When the above paragraph is properly arranged, it ends with the words 5.____
   A. "...and protection." B. "...the United States."
   C. "...their safeguards." D. "...in Great Britain."
   E. "...chemical fields."

KEY (CORRECT ANSWERS)

1. C
2. C
3. D
4. A
5. C

TEST 2

DIRECTIONS: In each of the questions numbered I through V, several sentences are given. For each question, choose as your answer the group of number that represents the MOST logical order of these sentences if they were arranged in paragraph form. *PRINT THE LETTER OF THE CORRECT ANSWER IN THE SPACE AT THE RIGHT.*

1. I. It is established when one shows that the landlord has prevented the tenant's enjoyment of his interest in the property leased. 1.____
   II. Constructive eviction is the result of a breach of the covenant of quiet enjoyment implied in all leases.
   III. In some parts of the United States, it is not complete until the tenant vacates within a reasonable time.
   IV. Generally, the acts must be of such serious and permanent character as to deny the tenant the enjoyment of his possessing rights.
   V. In this event, upon abandonment of the premises, the tenant's liability for that ceases.

   The CORRECT answer is:
   A. II, I, IV, III, V
   B. V, II, III, I, IV
   C. IV, III, I, II, V
   D. I, III, V, IV, II

2. I. The powerlessness before private and public authorities that is the typical experience of the slum tenant is reminiscent of the situation of blue-collar workers all through the nineteenth century. 2.____
   II. Similarly, in recent years, this chapter of history has been reopened by anti-poverty groups which have attempted to organize slum tenants to enable them to bargain collectively with their landlords about the conditions of their tenancies.
   III. It is familiar history that many of the worker remedied their condition by joining together and presenting their demands collectively.
   IV. Like the workers, tenants are forced by the conditions of modern life into substantial dependence on these who possess great political aid and economic power.
   V. What's more, the very fact of dependence coupled with an absence of education and self-confidence makes them hesitant and unable to stand up for what they need from those in power.

   The CORRECT answer is:
   A. V, IV, I, II, III
   B. II, III, I, V, IV
   C. III, I, V, IV, II
   D. I, IV, V, III, II

3. I. A railroad, for example, when not acting as a common carrier may contract away responsibility for its own negligence. 3.____
   II. As to a landlord, however, no decision has been found relating to the legal effect of a clause shifting the statutory duty of repair to the tenant.
   III. The courts have not passed on the validity of clauses relieving the landlord of this duty and liability.
   IV. They have, however, upheld the validity of exculpatory clauses in other types of contracts.

V. Housing regulations impose a duty upon the landlord to maintain leased premises in safe condition.
VI. As another example, a bailee may limit his liability except for gross negligence, willful acts, or fraud.

The CORRECT answer is:
A. II, I, VI, IV, III, V
B. I, III, IV, V, VI, II
C. III, V, I, IV, II, VI
D. V, III, IV, I, VI, II

4. I. Since there are only samples in the building, retail or consumer sales are generally eschewed by mart occupants, and in some instances, rigid controls are maintained to limit entrance to the mart only to those persons engaged in retailing. 4.____
II. Since World War I, in many larger cities, there has developed a new type of property, called the mart building.
III. It can, therefore, be used by wholesalers and jobbers for the display of sample merchandise.
IV. This type of building is most frequently a multi-storied, finished interior property which is a cross between a retail arcade and a loft building.
V. This limitation enables the mart occupants to ship the orders from another location after the retailer or dealer makes his selection from the samples.

The CORRECT answer is:
A. II, IV, III, I, V
B. IV, III, V, I, II
C. I, III, II, IV, V
D. I, IV, II, III, V

5. I. In general, staff-line friction reduces the distinctive contribution of staff personnel. 5.____
II. The conflicts, however, introduce an uncontrolled element into the managerial system.
III. On the other hand, the natural resistance of the line to staff innovations probably usefully restrains over-eager efforts to apply untested procedures on a large scale.
IV. Under such conditions, it is difficult to know when valuable ideas are being sacrificed.
V. The relatively weak position of staff, requiring accommodation to the line, tends to restrict their ability to engage in free, experimental innovation.

The CORRECT answer is:
A. IV, II, III, I, V
B. I, V, III, II, IV
C. V, III, I, II, IV
D. II, I, IV, V, III

KEY (CORRECT ANSWERS)

1. A
2. D
3. D
4. A
5. B

TEST 3

DIRECTIONS: Questions 1 through 4 consist of six sentences which can be arranged in a logical sequence. For each question, select the choice which places the numbered sentences in the MOST logical sequent. *PRINT THE LETTER OF THE CORRECT ANSWER IN THE SPACE AT THE RIGHT.*

1. I. The burden of proof as to each issue is determined before trial and remains upon the same party throughout the trial. 1.____
   II. The jury is at liberty to believe one witness' testimony as against a number of contradictory witnesses.
   III. In a civil case, the party bearing the burden of proof is required to prove his contention by a fair preponderance of the evidence.
   IV. However, it must be noted that a fair preponderance of evidence does not necessarily mean a greater number of witnesses.
   V. The burden of proof is the burden which rests upon one of the parties to an action to persuade the trier of the facts, generally the jury, that a proposition he asserts is true.
   VI. If the evidence is equally balanced, or if it leaves the jury in such doubt as to be unable to decide the controversy either way, judgment must be given against the party upon whom the burden of proof rests.

   The CORRECT answer is:
   A. III, II, V, IV, I, VI
   B. I, II, VI, V, III, IV
   C. III, IV, V, I, II, VI
   D. V, I, III, VI, IV, II

2. I. If a parent is without assets and is unemployed, he cannot be convicted of the crime of non-support of a child. 2.____
   II. The term "sufficient ability" has been held to mean sufficient financial ability.
   III. It does not matter if his unemployment is by choice or unavoidable circumstances.
   IV. If he fails to take any steps at all, he may be liable to prosecution for endangering the welfare of a child.
   V. Under the penal law, a parent is responsible for the support of his minor child only if the parent is "of sufficient ability."
   VI. An indigent parent may meet his obligation by borrowing money or by seeking aid under the provisions of the Social Welfare Law.

   The CORRECT answer is:
   A. VI, I, V, III, II, IV
   B. I, III, V, II, IV, VI
   C. V, II, I, III, VI, IV
   D. I, VI, IV, V, II, III

3. I. Consider, for example, the case of a rabble rouser who urges a group of twenty people to go out and break the windows of a nearby factory. 3.____
   II. Therefore, the law fills the indicated gap with the crime of inciting to riot.
   III. A person is considered guilty of inciting to riot when he urges ten or more persons to engage in tumultuous and violent conduct of a kind likely to create public alarm.
   IV. However, if he has not obtained the cooperation of at least four people, he cannot be charged with unlawful assembly.

V. The charge of inciting to riot was added to the law to cover types of conduct which cannot be classified as either the crime of "riot" or the crime of "unlawful assembly."
VI. If he acquires the acquiescence of at least four of them, he is guilty of unlawful assembly even if the project does not materialize.

The CORRECT answer is:
A. III, V, I, VI, IV, II
B. V, I, IV, VI, II, III
C. III, IV, I, V, II, VI
D. V, I, IV, VI, III, II

4. I. If, however, the rebuttal evidence presents an issue of credibility, it is for the jury to determine whether the presumption has, in fact, been destroyed. 4.____
II. Once sufficient evidence to the contrary is introduced, the presumption disappears from the trial.
III. The effect of a presumption is to place the burden upon the adversary to come forward with evidence to rebut the presumption.
IV. When a presumption is overcome and ceases to exist in the case, the fact or facts which gave rise to the presumption still remain.
V. Whether a presumption has been overcome is ordinarily a question for the court.
VI. Such information may furnish a basis for a logical inference.

The CORRECT answer is:
A. IV, VI, II, V, I, III
B. III, II, V, I, IV, VI
C. V, III, VI, IV, II, I
D. V, IV, I, II, VI, III

KEY (CORRECT ANSWERS)

1. D
2. C
3. A
4. B

PREPARING WRITTEN MATERIAL

EXAMINATION SECTION

TEST 1

DIRECTIONS: The following groups of sentences need to be arranged in an order that makes sense. Select the letter preceding the sequence that represents the BEST sentence order. *PRINT THE LETTER OF THE CORRECT ANSWER IN THE SPACE AT THE RIGHT.*

1. I. A large Naval station on Alameda Island, near Oakland, held many warships in port, and the War Department was worried that if the bridge were to be blown up by the enemy, passage to and from the bay would be hopelessly blocked. 1.____
   II. Though many skeptics were opposed to the idea of building such an enormous bridge, the most vocal opposition came from a surprising source: the United States War Department.
   III. The War Department's concerns led to a showdown at San Francisco City Hall between Strauss and the Secretary of War, who demanded to know what would happen if a military enemy blew up the bridge.
   IV. In 1933, by submitting a construction cost estimate of $17 million, an engineer named Joseph Strauss won the contract to build the Golden Gate Bridge of San Francisco, which would then become one of the world's largest bridges.
   V. Strauss quickly ended the debate by explaining that the Golden Gate Bridge was to be a suspension bridge, whose roadway would hang in the air from cables strung between two huge towers, and would immediately sink into three hundred feet of water if it were destroyed.

   The BEST order is:
   A. II, III, I, IV, V B. I, II, III, V, IV C. IV, II, I, III, V D. IV, I, III, V, II

2. I. Plastic surgeons have already begun to use virtual reality to map out the complex nerve and tissue structures of a particular patient's face, in order to prepare for delicate surgery. 2.____
   II. A virtual reality program responds to these movements by adjusting the images that a person sees on a screen or through goggles, thereby creating an "interactive" world in which a person can see and touch three-dimensional graphic objects.
   III. No more than a computer program that is designed to build and display graphic images, the virtual reality program takes graphic programs a step further by sensing a person's head and body movements.
   IV. The computer technology known as virtual reality, now in its very first stages of development, is already revolutionizing some aspects of contemporary life.
   V. Virtual reality computers are also being used by the space program, most recently to simulate conditions for the astronauts who were launched on a repair mission to the Hubble telescope.

The BEST order is:
A. IV, II, I, V, III B. III, I, V, II, IV C. IV, III, II, I, V D. III, I, II, IV, V

3. I. Before you plant anything, the soil in your plant bed should be carefully raked level, a small section at a time, and any clods or rocks that can't be broken up should be removed. 3.____
II. Your plant should be placed in a hole that will position it at the same level it was at the nursery, and a small indentation should be pressed into the soil around the plant in order to hold water near its roots.
III. Before placing the plant in the soil, lightly separate any roots that may have been matted together in the container, cutting away any thick masses that can't be separated, so that the remaining roots will be able to grow outward.
IV. After the bed is ready, remove your plant from its container by turning it upside down and tapping or pushing on the bottom —never remove it by pulling on the plant.
V. When you bring home a small plant in an individual container from the nursery, there are several things to remember while preparing to plant it in your own garden.

The BEST order is:
A. V, IV, III, II, I B. V, II, IV, III, II C. I, IV, II, III, V D. I, IV, V, II, III

4. I. The motte and its tower were usually built first, so that sentries could use it as a lookout to warn the castle workers of any danger that might approach the castle. 4.____
II. Though the moat and palisade offered the bailey a good deal of protection, it was linked to the motte by a set of stairs that led to a retractable drawbridge at the motte's gate, to enable people to evacuate onto the motte in case of an attack.
III. The motte of these early castles was a fortified hill, sometimes as high as one hundred feet, on which stood a palisade and tower.
IV. The bailey was a clear, level spot below the motte, also enclosed by a palisade, which in turn was surrounded by a large trench or moat.
V. The earliest castles built in Europe were not the magnificent stone giants that still tower over much of the European landscape, but simpler wooden constructions called motte-and-bailey castles.

The BEST order is:
A. V, III, I, IV, II B. V, IV, I, II, III C. I, IV, III, II, V D. I, III, II, IV, V

5. I. If an infant is left alone or abandoned for a short while, its immediate response is to cry loudly, accompanying its screams with aggressive flailing of its legs and limbs. 5.____
II. If a child has been abandoned for a longer period of time, it becomes completely still and quiet, as if realizing that now its only chance for survival is to shut its mouth and remain motionless.
III. Along with their intense fear of the dark, the crying behavior of human infants offers insights into how prehistoric newborn children might have evolved instincts that would prevent them from becoming victims of predators.

IV. This behavior often surprises people who enter a hospital's maternity ward for the first time and encounter total silence from a roomful of infants.
V. This violent screaming response is quite different from an infant's cries of discomfort or hunger, and seems to serve as either the child's first line of defense against an unwanted intruder, or a desperate attempt to communicate its position to the mother.

The BEST order is:
A. III, II, IV, I, V B. III, I, V, II, IV C. I, V, IV, II, III D. II, IV, I, V, III

6. I. When two cats meet who are strangers, their first actions and gestures determine who the "dominant" cat will be, at least for the time being. 6.____
II. Unlike dogs, cats are typically a solitary animal species who avoid social interaction, but they do display specific social responses to each other upon meeting.
III. This is unlikely, however; before such a point of open hostility is reached, one of the cats will usually take the "submissive" position of crouching down while looking away from the other dat.
IV. If a cat desires dominance or sees the other cat as a threat to its territory, it will stare directly at the intruder with a lowered tail.
V. If the other cat responds with a similar gesture, or with the strong defensive posture of an arched back, laid-back ears and raised tail, a fight or chase is likely if neither cat gives in.

The BEST order is:
A. IV, II, I, V, III B. I, II, IV, V, III C. I, IV, V, III, II D. II, I, IV, V, III

7. I. A star or planet's gravitational force can best be explained in this way: anything passing through this "dent" in space will veer toward the star or planet as if it were rolling into a hole. 7.____
II. Objects that are massive or heavy, such as stars or planets, "sink" into this surface, creating a sort of dent or concavity in the surrounding space.
III. Black holes, the most massive objects known to exist in space, create dents so large and deep that the space surrounding them actually folds in on itself, preventing anything that falls in —even light —from ever escaping again.
IV. The sort of dent a star or planet makes depends on how massive it is; planets generally have weak gravitational pulls, but stars, which are larger and heavier, make a bigger "dent" that will attract more matter.
V. In outer space, the force of gravity works as if the surrounding space is a soft, flat surface.

The BEST order is:
A. III, V, II, I, IV B. III, IV, I, V, II C. V, II, I, IV, III D. I, V, II, IV, III

8. I. Eventually, the society of Kyoto gave the world one of its first and greatest novels when Japan's most promising writer, Lady Murasaki Shikibu, wrote her chronicle of Kyoto's society, *The Tale of Genji*, which preceded the first European novels by more than 500 years. 8.____
II. The society of Kyoto was dedicated to the pleasures of art; the courtiers experimented with new and colorful methods of sculpture, painting, writing, decorative gardening, and even making clothes.

III. Japanese culture began under the powerful authority of Chinese Buddhism, which influenced every aspect of Japanese life from religion to politics and art.
IV. This new, vibrant culture was so sophisticated that all the people in Kyoto's imperial court considered themselves poets, and the line between life and art hardly existed —lovers corresponded entirely through written verses, and even government officials communicated by writing poems to each other.
V. In the eighth century, when the emperor established the town of Kyoto as the capital of the Japanese empire, Japanese society began to develop its own distinctive style.

The BEST order is:
A. V, II, IV, I, III B. II, I, V, IV, III C. V, III, IV, I, II D. III, V, II, IV, I

9. I. Instead of wheels, the HSST uses two sets of magnets, one which sits on the track, and another that is carried by the train; these magnets generate an identical magnetic field which forces the two sets apart. 9.____
II. In the last few decades, railway travel has become less popular throughout the world, because it is much slower than travel by airplane, and not much less expensive.
III. The HSST's designers say that the train can take passengers from one town to another as quickly as a jet plane —while consuming less than half the energy.
IV. This repellent effect is strong enough to lift the entire train above the trackway, and the train, literally traveling on air, rockets along at speeds of up to 300 miles per hour.
V. The revolutionary technology of magnetic levitation, currently being tested by Japan's experimental HSST (High Speed Surface Transport), may yet bring passenger trains back from the dead.

The BEST order is:
A. II, V, I, IV, III B. II, I, IV, III, V C. V, II, III, I, IV D. V, I, III, IV, II

10. I. When European countries first began to colonize the African continent, their impression of the African people was of a vast group of loosely organized tribal societies, without any great centralized source of power or wealth. 10.____
II. The legend of Timbuktu persisted until the nineteenth century, when a French adventurer visited Timbuktu and found that raids by neighboring tribesmen had made the city a shadow of its former self.
III. In the fifteenth century, when the stories of travelers who had traveled Africa's Sudan region began circulating around Europe, this impression began to change.
IV. In 1470, an Italian merchant named Benedetto Dei traveled to Timbuktu and confirmed these rumors, describing a thriving metropolis where rich and poor people worshipped together in the city's many ornate mosques — there was even a university in Timbuktu, much like its European counterparts, where African scholars pursued their studies in the arts and sciences.

V. The travelers' legends told of an enormous city in the western Sudan, Timbuktu, where the streets were crowded with goods brought by faraway caravans, and where there was a stone palace as large as any in Europe.

The BEST order is:

A. III, V, I, IV, II B. I, II, IV, III, V C. I, III, V, IV, II D. II, I, III, IV, V

11. I. Also, our reference points in sighting the moon make us believe that its size is changing; when the moon is rising through the trees, it seems huge, because our brains unconsciously compare the size of the moon with the size of the trees in the foreground. 11.____

II. To most people, the sky itself appears more distant at the horizon than directly overhead, and if the moon's size—which remains constant—is projected from the horizon, the apparent distance of the horizon makes the moon look bigger.

III. Up higher in the sky, the moon is set against tiny stars in the background, which will make the moon seem smaller.

IV. People often wonder why the moon becomes bigger when it approaches the horizon, but most scientists agree that this is a complicated optical illusion, produced by at least three factors.

V. The moon illusion may also be partially explained by a phenomenon that has nothing to do with errors in our perception—light that enters the earth's atmosphere is sometimes refracted, and so the atmosphere may act as a kind of magnifying glass for the moon's image.

The BEST order is:

A. IV, III, V, II, I B. IV, II, I, III, V C. V, II, I, III, IV D. II, I, III, IV, V

12. I. When the Native Americans were introduced to the horses used by white explorers, they were amazed at their new alternative—here was an animal that was strong and swift, would patiently carry a person or other loads on its back, and they later discovered, was right at home on the plains. 12.____

II. Before the arrival of European explorers to North America, the natives of the American plains used large dogs to carry their travois-long lodgepoles loaded with clothing, gear, and food.

III. These horses, it is now known, were not really strangers to North America; the very first horses originated here, on this continent, tens of thousands of years ago, and migrated into Asia across the Bering Land Bridge, a strip of land that used to link our continent with the Eastern world.

IV. At first, the natives knew so little about horses that at least one tribe tried to feed their new animals pieces of dried meat and animal fat, and were surprised when the horses turned their heads away and began to eat the grass of the prairie.

V. The American horse eventually became extinct, but its Asian cousins were reintroduced to the New World when the European explorers brought them to live among the Native Americans.

The BEST order is:

A. II, I, IV, III, V B. II, IV, I, III, V C. I, II, IV, III, V D. I, III, V, II, IV

13. I. The dress worn by the dancer is believed to have been adorned in the past by shells which would strike each other as the dancer performed, creating a lovely sound. 13.____
II. Today's jingle-dress is decorated with the tin lids of snuff cans, which are rolled into cones and sewn onto the dress,
III. During the jingle-dress dance, the dancer must blend complicated footwork with a series of gentle hos that cause the cones to jingle in rhythm to a drumbeat.
IV. When contemporary Native American tribes meet for a pow-wow, one of the most popular ceremonies to take place is the women's jingle-dress dance.
V. Besides being more readily available than shells, the lids are thought by many dancers to create a softer, more subtle sound.
The BEST order is:
A. II, IV, V, I, III B. IV, II, I, III, V C. II, I, III, V, IV D. IV, I, II, V, III

14. I. If a homeowner lives where seasonal climates are extreme, deciduous shade trees—which will drop their leaves in the winter and allow sunlight to pass through the windows—should be planted near the southern exposure in order to keep the house cool during the summer. 14.____
II. This trajectory is shorter and lower in the sky than at any other time of year during the winter, when a house most requires heating; the northern-facing parts of a house do not receive any direct sunlight at all.
III. In designing an energy-efficient house, especially in colder climates, it is important to remember that most of the house's windows should face south.
IV. Though the sun always rises in the east and sets in the west, the sun of the northern hemisphere is permanently situated in the southern portion of the sky.
V. The explanation for why so many architects and builders want this "southern exposure" is related to the path of the sun in the sky.
The BEST order is:
A. III, I, V, IV, II B. III, V, IV, II, I C. I, III, IV, II, V D. I, II, V, IV, III

15. I. His journeying lasted twenty-four years and took him over an estimated 75,000 miles, a distance that would not be surpassed by anyone other than Magellan—who sailed around the world—for another six hundred years. 15.____
II. Perhaps the most far-flung of these lesser-known travelers was Ibn Batuta, an African Moslem who left his birthplace of Tangier in the summer of 1325.
III. Ibn Batuta traveled all over Africa and Asia, from Niger to Peking, and to the islands of Maldive and Indonesia.
IV. However, a few explorers of the Eastern world logged enough miles and adventures to make Marco Polo's voyage look like an evening stroll.
V. In America, the most well-known of the Old World's explorers are usually Europeans such as Marco Polo, the Italian who brought many elements of Chinese culture to the Western world.
The BEST order is:
A. V, IV, II, III, I B. V, IV, III, II, I C. III, II, I, IV, V D. II, III, I, IV, V

16. I. In the rainforests of South America, a rare species of frog practices a reproductive method that is entirely different from this standard process. 16.____
    II. She will eventually carry each of the tadpoles up into the canopy and drop each into its own little pool, where it will be easy to locate and safe from most predators.
    III. After fertilization, the female of the species, who lives almost entirely on the forest floor, lays between 2 and 16 eggs among the leaf litter at the base of a tree, and stands watch over these eggs until they hatch.
    IV. Most frogs are pond-dwellers who are able to deposit hundreds of eggs in the water and then leave them alone, knowing that enough eggs have been laid to insure the survival of some of their offspring.
    V. Once the tadpoles emerge, the female backs in among them, and a tadpole will wriggle onto her back to be carried high into the forest canopy, where the female will deposit it in a little pool of water cupped in the leaf of a plant.

    The BEST order is:
    A. I, IV, III, II, V B. I, III, V, II, IV C. IV, III, II, V, I D. IV, I, III, V, II

17. I. Eratosthenes had heard from travelers that at exactly noon on June 21, in the ancient city of Aswan, Egypt, the sun cast no shadow in a well, which meant that the sun must be directly overhead. 17.____
    II. He knew the sun always cast a shadow in Alexandria, and so he figured that if he could measure the length of an Alexandria shadow at the time when there was no shadow in Aswan, he could calculate the angle of the sun, and therefore the circumference of the earth.
    III. The evidence for a round earth was not new in 1492; in fact, Eratosthenes, an Alexandrian geographer who lived nearly sixteen centuries before Columbus's voyage (275-195 B.C.), actually developed a method for calculating the circumference of the earth that is still in use today.
    IV. Eratosthenes's method was correct, but his result—28,700 miles—was about 15 percent too high, probably because of the inaccurate ancient methods of keeping time, and because Aswan was not due south of Alexandria, as Eratosthenes had believed.
    V. When Christopher Columbus sailed across the Atlantic Ocean for the first time in 1492, there were still some people in the world who ignored scientific evidence and believed that the earth was flat, rather than round.

    The BEST order is:
    A. I, II, V, III, IV B. V, III, IV, I, II C. V, III, I, II, IV D. III, V, I, II, IV

18. I. The first name for the child is considered a trial naming, often impersonal and neutral, such as the Ngoni name *Chabwera*, meaning "it has arrived." 18.____
    II. This sort of name is not due to any parental indifference to the child, but is a kind of silent recognition of Africa's sometimes high infant death rate; most parents ease the pain of losing a child with the belief that it is not really a person until it has been given a final name.
    III. In many tribal African societies, families often give two different names to their children, at different periods in time.
    IV. After the trial naming period has subsided and it is clear that the child will survive, the parents choose a final name for the child, an act that symbolically completes the act of birth.

V. In fact, some African first-given names are explicitly uncomplimentary, translating as "I am dead" or "I am ugly," in order to avoid the jealousy of ancestral spirits who might wish to take a child that is especially healthy or attractive.

The BEST order is:

A. III, I, II, V, IV B. III, IV, II, I, V C. IV, III, I, II, V D. IV, V, III, I, II

19. I. Though uncertain of the definite reasons for this behavior, scientists believe the birds digest the clay in order to counteract toxins contained in the seeds of certain fruits that are eaten by macaws. 19.____

II. For example, all macaws flock to riverbanks at certain times of the year to eat the clay that is found in river mud.

III. The macaws of South America are not only among the largest and most beautifully colored of the world's flying birds, but they are also one of the smartest.

IV. It is believed that macaws are forced to resort to these toxic fruits during the dry season, when foods are more scarce.

V. The macaw's intelligence has led to intense study by scientists, who have discovered some macaw behaviors that have not yet been explained.

The BEST order is:

A. III, IV, I, II, V B. III, V, II, I, IV C. V, II, I, IV, III D. IV, I, II, III, V

20. I. Although Maggie Kuhn has since passed away, the Gray Panthers are still waging a campaign to reinstate the historical view of the elderly as people whose experience allows them to make their greatest contribution in their later years. 20.____

II. In 1972, an elderly woman named Maggie Kuhn responded to this sort of treatment by forming a group called the Gray Panthers, an organization of both old and young adults with the common goal of creating change.

III. This attitude is reflected strongly in the way elderly people are treated by our society; many are forced into early retirement, or are placed in rest homes in which they are isolated from their communities.

IV. Unlike most other cultures around the world, Americans tend to look upon old age with a sense of dread and sadness.

V. Kuhn believed that when the elderly are forced to withdraw into lives that lack purpose, society loses one of its greatest resources: people who have a lifetime of experience and wisdom to offer their communities.

The BEST order is:

A. IV, III, II, V, I B. IV, II, I, III, V C. II, IV, III, V, I D. II, I, IV, III, V

21. I. The current theory among most anthropologists is that humans evolved from apes who lived in trees near the grasslands of Africa. 21.____

II. Still, some anthropologists insist that such an invention was necessary for the survival of early humans, and point to the Kung Bushmen of central Africa as a society in which the sling is still used in this way.

III. Two of these inventions—fire, and weapons such as spears and clubs—were obvious defenses against predators, and there is archaeological evidence to support the theory of their use.

IV. Once people had evolved enough to leave the safety of trees and walk upright, they needed the protection of several inventions in order to survive.
V. But another invention, a feather or fiber sling that allowed mothers to carry children while leaving their hands free to gather roots or berries, would certainly have decomposed and left behind no trace of itself.

The BEST order is:
A. I, II, III, V, IV B. IV, I, II, III, V C. I, IV, III, V, II D. IV, III, V, II, I

22. I. The person holding the bird should keep it in hot water up to its neck, and the person cleaning should work a mild solution of dishwashing liquid into the bird's plumage, paying close attention to the head and neck. 22.____
II. When rinsing the bird, after all the oil has been removed, the running water should be directed against the lay of its feathers, until water begins to bead off the surface of the feathers—a sign that all the detergent has been rinsed out.
III. If you have rescued a sea bird from an oil spill and want to restore it to clean and normal living, you need a large sink, a constant supply of running hot water (a little over 100ºF), and regular dishwashing liquid.
IV. This cleaning with detergent solution should be repeated as many times as it takes to remove all traces of oil from the bird's feathers, sometime over a period of several days.
V. But before you begin to clean the bird, you must find a partner because cleaning an oiled bird is a two-person job.

The BEST order is:
A. III, I, II, IV, V B. III, V, I, IV, II C. III, I, IV, V, II D. III, IV, V, I, II

23. I. The most difficult time of year for the Tsaatang is the spring calving, when the reindeer leave their wintering ground and rush to their accustomed calving place, without stopping by night or by day. 23.____
II. Reindeer travel in herds, and though some animals are tamed by the Tsaatang for riding or milking, the herds are allowed to roam free.
III. This journey is hard for the Tsaatang, who carry all their possessions with them, but once it's over it proves worthwhile; the Tsaatang can immediately begin to gather milk from reindeer cows who have given birth.
IV. The Tsaatang, a small tribe who live in the far northwest corner of Mongolia, practice a lifestyle that is completely dependent on the reindeer, their main resource for food, clothing, and transport.
V. The people must follow their yearly migrations, living in portable shelters that resemble Native American tepees.

The BEST order is:
A. I, III, II, V, IV B. I, IV, II, V, III C. IV, I, III, V, II D. IV II, V, I, III

24. I. The Romans later improved this system by installing these heated pipe networks throughout walls and ceilings, supplying heat to even the uppermost floors of a building—a system that, to this day, hasn't been much improved. 24.____
II. Air-conditioning, the method by which humans control indoor temperatures, was practiced much earlier than most people think.

III. The earliest heating devices other than open fires were used in 350 B.C. by the ancient Greeks, who directed air that had been heated by underground fires into baked clay pipes that ran under the floor.

IV. Ironically, the first successful cooling system, patented in England in 1831, used fire as its main energy source—fires were lit in the attic of a building, creating an updraft of air that drew cool air into the building through ducts that had underground openings near the river Thames.

V. Cooling buildings was more of a challenge, and wasn't attempted until 1500: a water-based system, designed by Leonardo da Vinci, does not appear to have been successful, since it was never used again.

The BEST order is:

A. III, V, IV, I, II B. III, I, II, V, IV C. II, III, I, V, IV D. IV, II, III, I, V

25. I. Cold, dry air from Canada passes over the Rocky Mountains and sweeps down onto the plains, where it collides with warm, moist air from the waters of the Gulf of Mexico, and when the two air masses meet, the resulting disturbance sometimes forms a violent funnel cloud that strikes the earth and destroys virtually everything in its path. 25.____

II. Hurricanes, storms which are generally not this violent and last much longer, are usually given names by meteorologists, but this tradition cannot be applied to tornados, which have a life span measured in minutes and disappear in the same way as they are born—unnamed.

III. A tornado funnel forms rotating columns of air whose speed reaches three hundred miles an hour—a speed that can only be estimated, because no wind-measuring devices in the direct path of a storm have ever survived.

IV. The natural phenomena known as tornados occur primarily over the Midwestern grasslands of the United States.

V. It is here, meteorologists tell us, that conditions for the formation of tornados are sometimes perfect during the spring months.

The BEST order is:

A. II IV, V, I, III B. II, III, I, V, IV C. IV, V, I, III, II D. IV, III, I, V, II

KEY (CORRECT ANSWERS)

1. C
2. C
3. B
4. A
5. B

6. D
7. C
8. D
9. A
10. C

11. B
12. A
13. D
14. B
15. A

16. D
17. C
18. A
19. B
20. A

21. C
22. B
23. D
24. C
25. C

PRINCIPLES AND PRACTICES, OF ADMINISTRATION, SUPERVISION AND MANAGEMENT

TABLE OF CONTENTS

PRINCIPLES AND PRACTICES, OF ADMINISTRATION, SUPERVISION AND MANAGEMENT

Most people are inclined to think of administration as something that only a few persons are responsible for in a large organization. Perhaps this is true if you are thinking of Administration with a capital *A*, but administration with a lower case *a* is a responsibility of supervisors at all levels each working day.

All of us feel we are pretty good supervisors and that we do a good job of administering the workings of our agency. By and large, this is true, but every so often it is good to check up on ourselves. Checklists appear from time to time in various publications which psychologists say tell whether or not a person will make a good wife, husband, doctor, lawyer, or supervisor.

The following questions are an excellent checklist to test yourself as a supervisor and administrator.

Remember, Administration gives direction and points the way but administration carries the ideas to fruition. Each is dependent on the other for its success. Remember, too, that no unit is too small for these departmental functions to be carried out. These statements apply equally as well to the Chief Librarian as to the Department Head with but one or two persons to supervise.

GENERAL ADMINISTRATION: General Responsibilities of Supervisors

1. Have I prepared written statements of functions, activities, and duties for my organizational unit?

2. Have I prepared procedural guides for operating activities?

3. Have I established clearly in writing, lines of authority and responsibility for my organizational unit?

4. Do I make recommendations for improvements in organization, policies, administrative and operating routines and procedures, including simplification of work and elimination of non-essential operations?

5. Have I designated and trained an understudy to function in my absence?

6. Do I supervise and train personnel within the unit to effectively perform their assignments?

7. Do I assign personnel and distribute work on such a basis as to carry out the organizational unit's assignment or mission in the most effective and efficient manner?

8. Have I established administrative controls by:

   a. Fixing responsibility and accountability on all supervisors under my direction for the proper performance of their functions and duties.

b. Preparations and submitting periodic work load and progress reports covering the operations of the unit to my immediate superior.

c. Analysis and evaluation of such reports received from subordinate units.

d. Submission of significant developments and problems arising within the organizational unit to my immediate superior.

e. Conducting conferences, inspections, etc., as to the status and efficiency of unit operations.

9. Do I maintain an adequate and competent working force?

10. Have I fostered good employee-department relations, seeing that established rules, regulations, and instructions are being carried out properly?

11. Do I collaborate and consult with other organizational units performing related functions to insure harmonious and efficient working relationships?

12. Do I maintain liaison through prescribed channels with city departments and other governmental agencies concerned with the activities of the unit?

13. Do I maintain contact with and keep abreast of the latest developments and techniques of administration (professional societies, groups, periodicals, etc.) as to their applicability to the activities of the unit?

14. Do I communicate with superiors and subordinates through prescribed organizational channels?

15. Do I notify superiors and subordinates in instances where bypassing is necessary as soon thereafter as practicable?

16. Do I keep my superior informed of significant developments and problems?

SEVEN BASIC FUNCTIONS OF THE SUPERVISOR

I. PLANNING
This means working out goals and means to obtain goals. What needs to be done, who will do it, how, when, and where it is to be done.

SEVEN STEPS IN PLANNING

A. Define job or problem clearly.
B. Consider priority of job.
C. Consider time-limit—starting and completing.
D. Consider minimum distraction to, or interference with, other activities.
E. Consider and provide for contingencies—possible emergencies.
F. Break job down into components.

G. Consider the 5 W's and H:
WHY..........is it necessary to do the job? (Is the purpose clearly defined?)
WHAT........needs to be done to accomplish the defined purpose?
.........is needed to do the job? (Money, materials, etc.)
WHO..........is needed to do the job?
..........will have responsibilities?
WHERE......is the work to be done?
WHEN........is the job to begin and end? (Schedules, etc.)
HOW..........is the job to bed done? (Methods, controls, records, etc.)

II. ORGANIZING

This means dividing up the work, establishing clear lines of responsibility and authority and coordinating efforts to get the job done.

III. STAFFING

The whole personnel function of bringing in and training staff, getting the right man and fitting him to the right job—the job to which he is best suited.

In the normal situation, the supervisor's responsibility regarding staffing normally includes providing accurate job descriptions, that is, duties of the jobs, requirements, education and experience, skills, physical, etc.; assigning the work for maximum use of skills; and proper utilization of the probationary period to weed out unsatisfactory employees.

IV. DIRECTING

Providing the necessary leadership to the group supervised. Important work gets done to the supervisor's satisfaction.

V. COORDINATING

The all-important duty of inter-relating the various parts of the work.
The supervisor is also responsible for controlling the coordinated activities. This means measuring performance according to a time schedule and setting quotas to see that the goals previously set are being reached. Reports from workers should be analyzed, evaluated, and made part of all future plans.

VI. REPORTING

This means proper and effective communication to your superiors, subordinates, and your peers (in definition of the job of the supervisor). Reports should be read and information contained therein should be used, not be filed away and forgotten. Reports should be written in such a way that the desired action recommended by the report is forthcoming.

VII. BUDGETING
This means controlling current costs and forecasting future costs. This forecast is based on past experience, future plans and programs, as well as current costs.

You will note that these seven functions can fall under three topics:

Planning) Organizing) Make a plan	Staffing) Directing) Controlling) Get things done	Reporting) Budgeting) Watch it work

PLANNING TO MEET MANAGEMENT GOALS

I. WHAT IS PLANNING?

A. Thinking a job through before new work is done to determine the best way to do it
B. A method of doing something
C. Ways and means for achieving set goals
D. A means of enabling a supervisor to deliver with a minimum of effort, all details involved in coordinating his work

II. WHO SHOULD MAKE PLANS?

Everybody!
All levels of supervision must plan work. (Top management, heads of divisions or bureaus, first line supervisors, and individual employees.) The higher the level, the more planning required.

III. WHAT ARE THE RESULTS OF POOR PLANNING?

A. Failure to meet deadline
B. Low employee morale
C. Lack of job coordination
D. Overtime is frequently necessary
E. Excessive cost, waste of material and manhours

IV. PRINCIPLES OF PLANNING

A. Getting a clear picture of your objectives. What exactly are you trying to accomplish?
B. Plan the whole job, then the parts, in proper sequence.
C. Delegate the planning of details to those responsible for executing them.
D. Make your plan flexible.
E. Coordinate your plan with the plans of others so that the work may be processed with a minimum of delay.
F. Sell your plan before you execute it.
G. Sell your plan to your superior, subordinate, in order to gain maximum participation and coordination.
H. Your plan should take precedence. Use knowledge and skills that others have brought to a similar job.
I. Your plan should take account of future contingencies; allow for future expansion.
J. Plans should include minor details. Leave nothing to chance that can be anticipated.
K. Your plan should be simple and provide standards and controls. Establish quality and quantity standards and set a standard method of doing the job. The controls will indicate whether the job is proceeding according to plan.
L. Consider possible bottlenecks, breakdowns, or other difficulties that are likely to arise.

V. Q. WHAT ARE THE YARDSTICKS BY WHICH PLANNING SHOULD BE MEASURED?

A. Any plan should:

—Clearly state a definite course of action to be followed and goal to be achieved, with consideration for emergencies.
— Be realistic and practical.
— State what's to be done, when it's to be done, where, how, and by whom.
— Establish the most efficient sequence of operating steps so that more is accomplished in less time, with the least effort, and with the best quality results.
— Assure meeting deliveries without delays.
— Establish the standard by which performance is to be judged.

Q. WHAT KINDS OF PLANS DOES EFFECTIVE SUPERVISION REQUIRE?

A. Plans should cover such factors as:

— Manpower: right number of properly trained employees on the job
— Materials: adequate supply of the right materials and supplies
— Machines: full utilization of machines and equipment, with proper maintenance
— Methods: most efficient handling of operations
— Deliveries: making deliveries on time
— Tools: sufficient well-conditioned tools
— Layout: most effective use of space
— Reports: maintaining proper records and reports
— Supervision: planning work for employees and organizing supervisor's own time

MANAGEMENT PRINCIPLES

I. MANAGEMENT

Q. What do we mean by management?

A. Getting work done through others.

Management could also be defined as planning, directing, and controlling the operations of a bureau or division so that all factors will function properly and all persons cooperate efficiently for a common objective.

II. MANAGEMENT PRINCIPLES

A. There should be a hierarchy—wherein authority and responsibility run upward and downward through several levels—with a broad base at the bottom and a single head at the top.

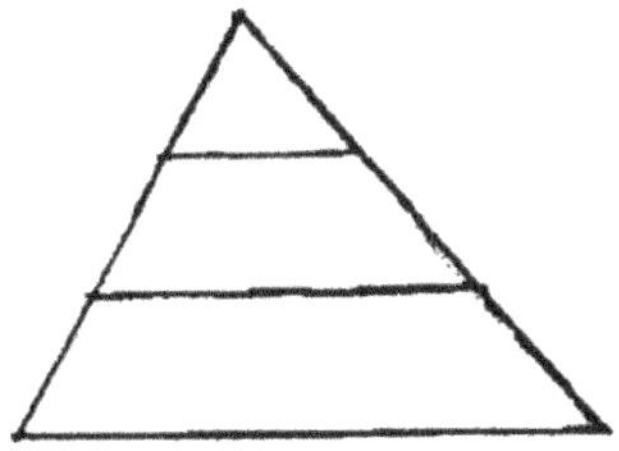

B. Each and every unit or person in the organization should be answerable ultimately to the manager at the apex. In other words, *The buck stops here!*

C. Every necessary function involved in the bureau's objectives is assigned to a unit in that bureau.

D. Responsibilities assigned to a unit are specifically clear-cut and understood.

E. Consistent methods of organizational structure should be applied at each level of the organization.

F. Each member of the bureau from top to bottom knows: to whom he reports and who reports to him.

G. No member of one bureau reports to more than one supervisor. No dual functions.

H. Responsibility for a function is matched by authority necessary to perform that function. Weight of authority.

I. Individuals or units reporting to a supervisor do not exceed the number which can be feasibly and effectively coordinated and directed. Concept of *span of control.*

J. Channels of command (management) are not violated by staff units, although there should be staff services to facilitate and coordinate management functions.

K. Authority and responsibility should be decentralized to units and individuals who are responsible for the actual performance of operations.
Welfare – down to Welfare Centers
Hospitals – down to local hospitals

L. Management should exercise control through attention to policy problems of exceptional performance, rather than through review of routine actions of subordinates.

M. Organizations should never be permitted to grow so elaborate as to hinder work accomplishments.

III. ORGANIZATION STRUCTURE

Types of Organizations
The purest form is a leader and a few followers, such as:

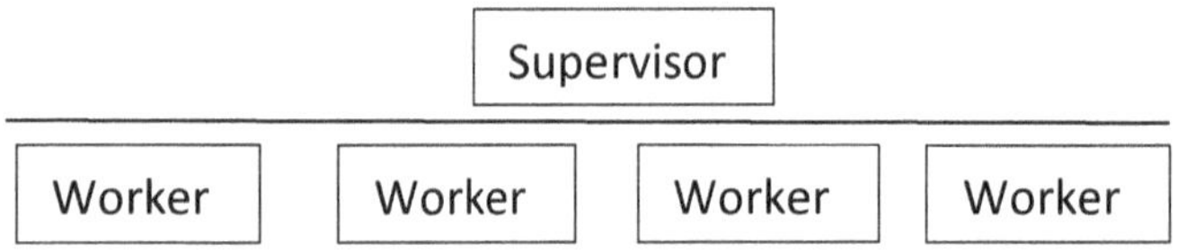

(Refer to organization chart) from supervisor to workers.

The line of authority is direct, The workers know exactly where they stand in relation to their boss, to whom they report for instructions and direction.

Unfortunately, in our present complex society, few organizations are similar to this example of a pure line organization. In this era of specialization, other people are often needed in the simplest of organizations. These specialists are known as staff. The sole purpose for their existence (staff) is to assist, advise, suggest, help or counsel line organizations. Staff has no authority to direct line people—nor do they give them direct instructions.

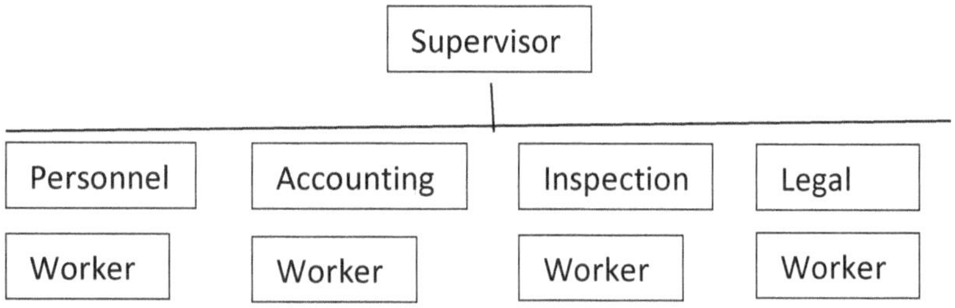

<u>Line Functions</u>

1. Directs
2. Orders
3. Responsibility for carrying out activities from beginning to end
4. Follows chain of command
5. Is identified with what it does
6. Decides when and how to use staff advice
7. Line executes

<u>Staff Functions</u>

1. Advises
2. Persuades and sells
3. Staff studies, reports, recommends but does not carry out
4. May advise across department lines
5. May find its ideas identified with others
6. Has to persuade line to want its advice
7. Staff: Conducts studies and research. Provides advice and instructions in technical matters. Serves as technical specialist to render specific services.

<u>Types and Functions of Organization Charts</u>

An organization chart is a picture of the arrangement and inter-relationship of the subdivisions of an organization.

A. Types of Charts:
   1. Structural: basic relationships only
   2. Functional: includes functions or duties
   3. Personnel: positions, salaries, status, etc.
   4. Process Chart: work performed
   5. Gantt Chart: actual performance against planned
   5. Flow Chart: flow and distribution of work

B. Functions of Charts:
   1. Assist in management planning and control
   2. Indicate duplication of functions
   3. Indicate incorrect stressing of functions
   4. Indicate neglect of important functions
   5. Correct unclear authority
   6. Establish proper span of control

C. Limitations of Charts:
1. Seldom maintained on current basis
2. Chart is oversimplified
3. Human factors cannot adequately be charted

D. Organization Charts should be:
1. Simple
2. Symmetrical
3. Indicate authority
4. Line and staff relationship differentiated
5. Chart should be dated and bear signature of approving officer
6. Chart should be displayed, not hidden

ORGANIZATION

There are four basic principles of organization:
1. Unity of command
2. Span of control
3. Uniformity of assignment
4. Assignment of responsibility and delegation of authority

I. UNITY OF COMMAND

Unity of command means that each person in the organization should receive orders from one, and only one, supervisor. When a person has to take orders from two or more people, (a) the orders may be in conflict and the employee is upset because he does not know which he should obey, or (b) different orders may reach him at the same time and he does not know which he should carry out first.

Equally as bad as having two bosses is the situation where the supervisor is bypassed. Let us suppose you are a supervisor whose boss bypasses you (deals directly with people reporting to you). To the worker, it is the same as having two bosses; but to you, the supervisor, it is equally serious. Bypassing on the part of your boss will undermine your authority, and the people under you will begin looking to your boss for decisions and even for routine orders.

You can prevent bypassing by telling the people you supervise that if anyone tries to give them orders, they should direct that person to you.

II. SPAN OF CONTROL

Span of control on a given level involves:
A. The number of people being supervised
B. The distance
C The time involved in supervising the people. (One supervisor cannot supervise too many workers effectively.)

Span of control means that a supervisor has the right number (not too many and not too few) of subordinates that he can supervise well.

III. UNIFORMITY OF ASSIGNMENT

In assigning work, you as the supervisor should assign to each person jobs that are similar in nature. An employee who is assigned too many different types of jobs will waste time in going from one kind of work to another. It takes time for him to get to top production in one kind of task and, before he does so, he has to start on another.
When you assign work to people, remember that:

A. Job duties should be definite. Make it clear from the beginning what they are to do, how they are to do it, and why they are to do it. Let them know how much they are expected to do and how well they are expected to do it.
B. Check your assignments to be certain that there are no workers with too many unrelated duties, and that no two people have been given overlapping responsibilities. Your aim should be to have every task assigned to a specific person with the work fairly distributed and with each person doing his part.

IV. ASSIGNMENT OF RESPONSIBILITY AND DELEGATION OF AUTHORITY

A supervisor cannot delegate his final responsibility for the work of his department. The experienced supervisor knows that he gets his work done through people. He can't do it all himself. So he must assign the work and the responsibility for the work to his employees. Then they must be given the authority to carry out their responsibilities.

By assigning responsibility and delegating authority to carry out the responsibility, the supervisor builds in his workers initiative, resourcefulness, enthusiasm, and interest in their work. He is treating them as responsible adults. They can find satisfaction in their work, and they will respect the supervisor and be loyal to the supervisor.

PRINCIPLES OF ORGANIZATION

I. DEFINITION

Organization is the method of dividing up the work to provide the best channels for coordinated effort to get the agency's mission accomplished.

II. PURPOSE OF ORGANIZATION

A. To enable each employee within the organization to clearly know his responsibilities and relationships to his fellow employees and to organizational units
B. To avoid conflicts of authority and overlapping of jurisdiction.
C. To ensure teamwork.

III. BASIC CONSIDERATIONS IIN ORGANIZATIONAL PLANNING

A. The basic plans and objectives of the agency should be determined, and the organizational structure should be adapted to carry out effectively such plans and objectives.
B. The organization should be built around the major functions of the agency and not individuals or groups of individuals.

C. The organization should be sufficiently flexible to meet new and changing conditions which may be brought about from within or outside the department.
D. The organizational structure should be as simple as possible and the number of organizational units kept at a minimum.
E. The number of levels of authority should be kept at a minimum. Each additional management level lengthens the chain of authority and responsibility and increases the time for instructions to be distributed to operating levels and for decisions to be obtained from higher authority.
F. The form of organization should permit each executive to exercise maximum initiative within the limits of delegated authority.

IV. BASES FOR ORGANIZATION

A. Purpose (Examples: education, police, sanitation)
B. Process (Examples: accounting, legal, purchasing)
C. Clientele (Examples: welfare, parks, veteran)
D. Geographic (Examples: borough offices, precincts, libraries)

V. ASSIGNMENTS OF FUNCTIONS

A. Every function of the agency should be assigned to a specific organizational unit. Under normal circumstances, no single function should be assigned to more than one organizational unit.
B. There should be no overlapping, duplication, or conflict between organizational elements.
C. Line functions should be separated from staff functions, and proper emphasis should be placed on staff activities.
D. Functions which are closely related or similar should normally be assigned to a single organizational unit.
E. Functions should be properly distributed to promote balance, and to avoid overemphasis of less important functions and underemphasis of more essential functions.

VI. DELEGATION OF AUTHORITY AND RESPONSIBILITY

A. Responsibilities assigned to a specific individual or organizational unit should carry corresponding authority, and all statements of authority or limitations thereof should be as specific as possible.
B. Authority and responsibility for action should be decentralized to organizational units and individuals responsible for actual performance to the greatest extent possible, without relaxing necessary control over policy or the standardization of procedures. Delegation of authority will be consistent with decentralization of responsibility but such delegation will not divest an executive in higher authority of his overall responsibility.
C. The heads of organizational units should concern themselves with important matters and should delegate to the maximum extent details and routines performed in the ordinary course of business.
D. All responsibilities, authorities, and relationships should be stated in simple language to avoid misinterpretation.
E. Each individual or organizational unit charged with a specific responsibility will be held responsible for results.

VII. EMPLOYEE RELATIONSHIPS

A. The employees reporting to one executive should not exceed the number which can be effectively directed and coordinated. The number will depend largely upon the scope and extent of the responsibilities of the subordinates.
B. No person should report to more than one supervisor. Every supervisor should know who reports to him, and every employee should know to whom he reports. Channels of authority and responsibility should not be violated by staff units.
C. Relationships between organizational units within the agency and with outside organizations and associations should be clearly stated and thoroughly understood to avoid misunderstanding.

DELEGATING

I. WHAT IS DELEGATING?
Delegating is assigning a job to an employee, giving him the authority to get that job done, and giving him the responsibility for seeing to it that the job is done.

A. What To Delegate
1. Routine details
2. Jobs which may be necessary and take a lot of time, but do not have to be done by the supervisor personally (preparing reports, attending meetings, etc.)
3. Routine decision-making (making decisions which do not require the supervisor's personal attention)

B. What Not To Delegate
1. Job details which are *executive functions* (setting goals, organizing employees into a good team, analyzing results so as to plan for the future)
2. Disciplinary power (handling grievances, preparing service ratings, reprimands, etc.)
3. Decision-making which involves large numbers of employees or other bureaus and departments
4. Final and complete responsibility for the job done by the unit being supervised

C. Why Delegate?
1. To strengthen the organization by developing a greater number of skilled employees
2. To improve the employee's performance by giving him the chance to learn more about the job, handle some responsibility, and become more interested in getting the job done
3. To improve a supervisor's performance by relieving him of routine jobs and giving him more time for *executive functions* (planning, organizing, controlling, etc.) which cannot be delegated

II. TO WHOM TO DELEGATE
People with abilities not being used. Selection should be based on ability, not on favoritism.

REPORTS

I. DEFINITION
A report is an orderly presentation of factual information directed to a specific reader for a specific purpose

II. PURPOSE
The general purpose of a report is to bring to the reader useful and factual information about a condition or a problem. Some specific purposes of a report may be:

A. To enable the reader to appraise the efficiency or effectiveness of a person or an operation
B. To provide a basis for establishing standards
C. To reflect the results of expenditures of time, effort, and money
D. To provide a basis for developing or altering programs

III. TYPES

A. Information Report: Contains facts arranged in sequence
B. Summary (Examination) Report: Contains facts plus an analysis or discussion of the significance of the facts. Analysis may give advantages and disadvantages or give qualitative and quantitative comparisons
C. Recommendation Report: Contains facts, analysis, and conclusion logically drawn from the facts and analysis, plus a recommendation based upon the facts, analysis, and conclusions

IV. FACTORS TO CONSIDER BEFORE WRITING REPORT

A. Why write the report?: The purpose of the report should be clearly defined.
B. Who will read the report?: What level of language should be used? Will the reader understand professional or technical language?
C. What should be said?: What does the reader need or want to know about the subject?
D. How should it be said?: Should the subject be presented tactfully? Convincingly? In a stimulating manner?

V. PREPARATORY STEPS

A. Assemble the facts: Find out who, why, what, where, when, and how.
B. Organize the facts: Eliminate unnecessary information
C. Prepare an outline: Check for orderliness, logical sequence
D. Prepare a draft: Check for correctness, clearness, completeness, conciseness, and tone
E. Prepare it in final form: Check for grammar, punctuation, appearance

VI. OUTLINE FOR A RECOMMENDATION REPORT

Is the report:
A. Correct in information, grammar, and tone?
B. Clear?
C. Complete?

D. Concise?
E. Timely?
F. Worth its cost?

Will the report accomplish its purpose?

MANAGEMENT CONTROLS

I. CONTROL
What is control? What is controlled? Who controls?

The essence of control is action which adjusts operations to predetermined standards, and its basis is information in the hands of managers. Control is checking to determine whether plans are being observed and suitable progress toward stated objectives is being made, and action is taken, if necessary, to correct deviations.

We have a ready-made model for this concept of control in the automatic systems which are widely used for process control in the chemical land petroleum industries. A process control system works this way. Suppose, for example, it is desired to maintain a constant rate of flow of oil through a pipe at a predetermined or set-point value. A signal, whose strength represents the rate of flow, can be produced in a measuring device and transmitted to a control mechanism. The control mechanism, when it detects any deviation of the actual from the set-point signal, will reposition the value regulating flow rate.

II. BASIS FOR CONTROL

A process control mechanism thus acts to adjust operations to predetermined standards and does so on the basis of information it receives. In a parallel way, information reaching a manager gives him the opportunity for corrective action and is his basis for control. He cannot exercise control without such information, and he cannot do a complete job of managing without controlling.

III. POLICY

What is policy?

Policy is simply a statement of an organization's intention to act in certain ways when specified types of circumstances arise. It represents a general decision, predetermined and expressed as a principle or rule, establishing a normal pattern of conduct for dealing with given types of business events—usually recurrent. A statement is therefore useful in economizing the time of managers and in assisting them to discharge their responsibilities equitably and consistently.

Policy is not a means of control, but policy does generate the need for control.

Adherence to policies is not guaranteed nor can it be taken on faith. It has to be verified. Without verification, there is no basis for control. Policy and procedures, although closely related and interdependent to a certain extent, are not synonymous. A policy may be adopted, for example, to maintain a materials inventory not to exceed one million dollars.

A procedure for inventory control could interpret that policy and convert it into methods for keeping within that limit, with consideration, too, of possible but foreseeable expedient deviation.

IV. PROCEDURE

What is procedure?

A procedure specifically prescribes:

A. What work is to be performed by the various participants
B. Who are the respective participants
C. When and where the various steps in the different processes are to be performed
D. The sequence of operations that will insure uniform handling of recurring transactions
E. The paper that is involved, its origin, transition, and disposition

Necessary appurtenances to a procedure are:

A. Detailed organizational chart
B. Flow charts
C. Exhibits of forms, all presented in close proximity to the text of the procedure

V. BASIS OF CONTROL – INFORMATION IN THE HANDS OF MANAGERS

If the basis of control is information in the hands of managers, then reporting is elevated to a level of very considerable importance.

Types of reporting may include:

A. Special reports and routine reports
B. Written, oral, and graphic reports
C. Staff meetings
D. Conferences
E. Television screens
F. Non-receipt of information, as where management is by exception
G. Any other means whereby information is transmitted to a manager as a basis for control action

FRAMEWORK OF MANAGEMENT

I. ELEMENTS

A. Policy: It has to be verified, controlled.

B. Organization is part of the giving of an assignment. The organizational chart gives to each individual in his title, a first approximation of the nature of his assignment and orients him as being accountable to a certain individual. Organization is not in a true sense a means of control. Control is checking to ascertain whether the assignment is executed as intended and acting on the basis of that information.

C. Budgets perform three functions:
   1. They present the objectives, plans, and programs of the organization in financial terms.

2. They report the progress of actual performance against these predetermined objectives, plans, and programs.
3. Like organizational charts, delegations of authority, procedures, and job descriptions, they define the assignments which have flowed from the Chief Executive. Budgets are a means of control in the respect that they report progress of actual performance against the program. They provide information which enables managers to take action directed toward bringing actual results into conformity with the program.

D. Internal Check provides in practice for the principle that the same person should not have responsibility for all phases of a transaction. This makes it clearly an aspect of organization rather than of control. Internal Check is static, or built-in.

E. Plans, Programs, Objectives
People must know what they are trying to do. Objectives fulfill this need. Without them, people may work industriously and yet, working aimlessly, accomplish little. Plans and Programs complement Objectives, since they propose how and according to what time schedule the objectives are to be reached.

F. Delegations of Authority
Among the ways we have for supplementing the titles and lines of authority of an organizational chart are delegations of authority. Delegations of authority clarify the extent of authority of individuals and in that way serve to define assignments. That they are not means of control is apparent from the very fact that wherever there has been a delegation of authority, the need for control increases. This could hardly be expected to happen if delegations of authority were themselves means of control.

II. MANAGER'S RESPONSIBILITY

Control becomes necessary whenever a manager delegates authority to a subordinate because he cannot delegate and then simply sit back and forget4 about it. A manager's accountability to his own superior has not diminished one whit as a result of delegating part of his authority to a subordinate. The manager must exercise control over actions taken under the authority so delegated. That means checking serves as a basis for possible corrective action.

Objectives, plans, programs, organizational charts, and other elements of the managerial system are not fruitfully regarded as either controls or means of control. They are pre-established standards or models of performance to which operations are adjusted by the exercise of management control. These standards or models of performance are dynamic in character for they are constantly altered, modified, or revised. Policies, organizational set-up, procedures, delegations, etc. are constantly altered but, like objectives and plans, they remain in force until they are either abandoned or revised. All of the elements (or standards or models of performance), objectives, plans, and programs, policies, organization, etc. can be regarded as a *framework of management*.

III. CONTROL TECHNIQUES

Examples of control techniques:

A. Compare against established standards
B. Compare with a similar operation
C. Compare with past operations
D. Compare with predictions of accomplishment

IV. WHERE FORECASTS FIT

Control is after-the-fact while forecasts are before. Forecasts and projections are important for setting objectives and formulating plans.

Information for aiming and planning does not have to be before-the-fact. It may be an after-the-fact analysis proving that a certain policy has been impolitic in its effect on the relation of the company or department with customer, employee, taxpayer, or stockholder; or that a certain plan is no longer practical, or that a certain procedure is unworkable.

The prescription here certainly would not be in control (in these cases, control would simply bring operations into conformity with obsolete standards) but the establishment of new standards, a new policy, a new plan, and a new procedure to be controlled too.

Information is, of course, the basis for all communication in addition to furnishing evidence to management of the need for reconstructing the framework of management.

PROBLEM SOLVING

The accepted concept in modern management for problem solving is the utilization of the following steps:

A. Identify the problem
B. Gather data
C. List possible solutions
D. Test possible solutions
E. Select the best solution
F. Put the solution into actual practice

Occasions might arise where you would have to apply the second step of gathering data before completing the first step.

You might also find that it will be necessary to work on several steps at the same time.

I. IDENTIFY THE PROBLEM

Your first step is to define as precisely as possible the problem to be solved. While this may sound easy, it is often the most difficult part of the process.

It has been said of problem solving that you are halfway to the solution when you can write out a clear statement of the problem itself.

Our job now is to get below the surface manifestations of the trouble and pinpoint the problem. This is usually accomplished by a logical analysis, by going from the general to the particular; from the obvious to the not-so-obvious cause.

Let us say that production is behind schedule. WHY? Absenteeism is high. Now, is absenteeism the basic problem to be tackled, or is it merely a symptom of low morale among the workforce? Under these circumstances, you may decide that production is not the problem; the problem is *employee morale*.

In trying to define the problem, remember there is seldom one simple reason why production is lagging, or reports are late, etc.

Analysis usually leads to the discovery that an apparent problem is really made up of several subproblems which must be attacked separately.

Another way is to limit the problem, and thereby ease the task of finding a solution, and concentrate on the elements which are within the scope of your control.

When you have gone this far, write out a tentative statement of the problem to be solved.

II. GATHER DATA

In the second step, you must set out to collect all the information that might have a bearing on the problem. Do not settle for an assumption when reasonable fact and figures are available.

If you merely go through the motions of problem-solving, you will probably shortcut the information-gathering step. Therefore, do not stack the evidence by confining your research to your own preconceived ideas.

As you collect facts, organize them in some form that helps you make sense of them and spot possible relationships between them. For example, plotting cost per unit figures on a graph can be more meaningful than a long column of figures.

Evaluate each item as you go along. Is the source material absolutely, reliable, probably reliable, or not to be trusted.

One of the best methods for gathering data is to go out and look the situation over carefully. Talk to the people on the job who are most affected by this problem.

Always keep in mind that a primary source is usually better than a secondary source of information.

III. LIST POSSIBLE SOLUTIONS

This is the creative thinking step of problem solving. This is a good time to bring into play whatever techniques of group dynamics the agency or bureau might have developed for a joint attack on problems.

Now the important thing for you to do is: Keep an open mind. Let your imagination roam freely over the facts you have collected. Jot down every possible solution that occurs to you. Resist the temptation to evaluate various proposals as you go along. List seemingly absurd ideas along with more plausible ones. The more possibilities you list during this step, the less risk you will run of settling for merely a workable, rather than the best, solution.

Keep studying the data as long as there seems to be any chance of deriving additional ideas, solutions, explanations, or patterns from it.

IV. TEST POSSIBLE SOLUTIONS

Now you begin to evaluate the possible solutions. Take pains to be objective. Up to this point, you have suspended judgment but you might be tempted to select a solution you secretly favored all along and proclaim it as the best of the lot.

The secret of objectivity in this phase is to test the possible solutions separately, measuring each against a common yardstick. To make this yardstick try to enumerate as many specific criteria as you can think of. Criteria are best phrased as questions which you ask of each possible solution. They can be drawn from these general categories:

Suitability – Will this solution do the job?
Will it solve the problem completely or partially?
Is it a permanent or a stopgap solution?

Feasibility - Will this plan work in actual practice?
Can we afford this approach?
How much will it cost?

Acceptability - Will the boss go along with the changes required in the plan?
Are we trying to drive a tack with a sledge hammer?

V. SELECT THE BEST SOLUTION

This is the area of executive decision.

Occasionally, one clearly superior solution will stand out at the conclusion of the testing process. But often it is not that simple. You may find that no one solution has come through all the tests with flying colors.

You may also find that a proposal, which flunked miserably on one of the essential tests, racked up a very high score on others.

The best solution frequently will turn out to be a combination.

Try to arrange a marriage that will bring together the strong points of one possible solution with the particular virtues of another. The more skill and imagination that you apply, the greater is the likelihood that you will come out with a solution that is not merely adequate and workable, but is the best possible under the circumstances.

VI. PUT THE SOLUTION INTO ACTUAL PRACTICE

As every executive knows, a plan which works perfectly on paper may develop all sorts of bugs when put into actual practice.

Problem-solving does not stop with selecting the solution which looks best in theory. The next step is to put the chosen solution into action and watch the results. The results may point towards modifications.

If the problem disappears when you put your solution into effect, you know you have the right solution.

If it does not disappear, even after you have adjusted your plan to cover unforeseen difficulties that turned up in practice, work your way back through the problem-solving solutions.

> Would one of them have worked better?
> Did you overlook some vital piece of data which would have given you a different slant on the whole situation? Did you apply all necessary criteria in testing solutions? If no light dawns after this much rechecking, it is a pretty good bet that you defined the problem incorrectly in the first place.

You came up with the wrong solution because you tackled the wrong problem.

Thus, step six may become step one of a new problem-solving cycle.

COMMUNICATION

I. WHAT IS COMMUNICATION?

We communicate through writing, speaking, action, or inaction. In speaking to people face-to-face, there is opportunity to judge reactions and to adjust the message. This makes the supervisory chain one of the most, and in many instances the most, important channels of communication.

In an organization, communication means keeping employees informed about the organization's objectives, policies, problems, and progress. Communication is the free interchange of information, ideas, and desirable attitudes between and among employees and between employees and management.

II. WHY IS COMMUNICATION NEEDED?

A. People have certain social needs
B. Good communication is essential in meeting those social needs
C. While people have similar basic needs, at the same time they differ from each other
D. Communication must be adapted to these individual differences

An employee cannot do his best work unless he knows why he is doing it. If he has the feeling that he is being kept in the dark about what is going on, his enthusiasm and productivity suffer.

Effective communication is needed in an organization so that employees will understand what the organization is trying to accomplish; and how the work of one unit contributes to or affects the work of other units in the organization and other organizations.

III. HOW IS COMMUNICATION ACHIEVED?

Communication flows downward, upward, sideways.

A. Communication may come from top management down to employees. This is downward communication.

Some means of downward communication are:
1. Training (orientation, job instruction, supervision, public relations, etc.)
2. Conferences
3. Staff meetings
4. Policy statements
5. Bulletins
6. Newsletters
7. Memoranda
8. Circulation of important letters

In downward communication, it is important that employees be informed in advance of changes that will affect them.

B. Communications should also be developed so that the ideas, suggestions, and knowledge of employees will flow upward to top management.

Some means of upward communication are:
1. Personal discussion conferences
2. Committees
3. Memoranda
4. Employees suggestion program
5. Questionnaires to be filled in giving comments and suggestions about proposed actions that will affect field operations.

Upward communication requires that management be willing to listen, to accept, and to make changes when good ideas are present. Upward communication succeeds when there is no fear of punishment for speaking out or lack of interest at the top. Employees will share their knowledge and ideas with management when interest is shown and recognition is given.

C. The advantages of downward communication:
1. It enables the passing down of orders, policies, and plans necessary to the continued operation of the station.
2. By making information available, it diminishes the fears and suspicions which result from misinformation and misunderstanding.
3. It fosters the pride people want to have in their work when they are told of good work.
4. It improves the morale and stature of the individual to be *in the know.*

5. It helps employees to understand, accept, and cooperate with changes when they know about them in advance.

D. The advantages of upward communication:
   1. It enables the passing upward of information, attitudes, and feelings.
   2. It makes it easier to find out how ready people are to receive downward communication.
   3. It reveals the degree to which the downward communication is understood and accepted.
   4. It helps to satisfy the basic social needs.
   5. It stimulates employees to participate in the operation of their organization.
   6. It encourage employees to contribute ideas for improving the efficiency and economy of operations.
   7. It helps to solve problem situations before they reach the explosion point.

IV. WHY DOES COMMUNICATION FAIL?

A. The technical difficulties of conveying information clearly
B. The emotional content of communication which prevents complete transmission
C. The fact that there is a difference between what management needs to say, what it wants to day, and what it does say
D. The fact that there is a difference between what employees would like to say, what they think is profitable or safe to say, and what they do say

V. HOW TO IMPROVE COMMUNICATION

As a supervisor, you are a key figure in communication. To improve as a communicator, you should:

A. Know: Knowing your subordinates will help you to recognize and work with individual differences.
B. Like: If you like those who work for you and those for whom you work, this will foster the kind of friendly, warm, work atmosphere that will facilitate communication.
C. Trust: Showing a sincere desire to communicate will help to develop the mutual trust and confidence which are essential to the free flow of communication.
D. Tell: Tell your subordinates and superiors *what's doing*. Tell your subordinates *why* as well as *how*.
E. Listen: By listening, you help others to talk and you create good listeners. Don't forget that listening implies action.
F. Stimulate: Communication has to be stimulated and encouraged. Be receptive to ideas and suggestions and motivate your people so that each member of the team identifies himself with the job at hand.
G. Consult: The most effective way of consulting is to let your people participate, insofar as possible, in developing determinations which affect them or their work.

VI. HOW TO DETERMINE WHETHER YOU ARE GETTING ACROSS

A. Check to see that communication is received and understood
B. Judge this understanding by actions rather than words
C. Adapt or vary communication, when necessary
D. Remember that good communication cannot cure all problems

VII. THE KEY ATTITUDE

Try to see things from the other person's point of view. By doing this, you help to develop the permissive atmosphere and the shared confidence and understanding which are essential to effective two-way communication.

Communication is a two-way process:
A. The basic purpose of any communication is to get action.
B. The only way to get action is through acceptance.
C. In order to get acceptance, communication must be humanly satisfying as well as technically efficient.

HOW ORDERS AND INSTRUCTIONS SHOULD BE GIVEN

I. CHARACTERISTICS OF GOOD ORDERS AND INSTRUCTIONS

A. Clear
Orders should be definite as to
—What is to be done
—Who is to do it
—When it is to be done
—Where it is to be done
—How it is to be done

B. Concise
Avoid wordiness. Orders should be brief and to the point.

C. Timely
Instructions and orders should be sent out at the proper time and not too long in advance of expected performance.

D. Possibility of Performance
Orders should be feasible:
1. Investigate before giving orders
2. Consult those who are to carry out instructions before formulating and issuing them

E. Properly Directed
Give the orders to the people concerned. Do not send orders to people who are not concerned. People who continually receive instructions that are not applicable to them get in the habit of neglecting instructions generally.

F. Reviewed Before Issuance
Orders should be reviewed before issuance:
1. Test them by putting yourself in the position of the recipient
2. If they involve new procedures, have the persons who are to do the work review them for suggestions.

G. Reviewed After Issuance
Persons who receive orders should be allowed to raise questions and to point out unforeseen consequences of orders.

H. Coordinated
Orders should be coordinated so that work runs smoothly.

I. Courteous
Make a request rather than a demand. There is no need to continually call attention to the fact that you are the boss.

J. Recognizable as an Order
Be sure that the order is recognizable as such.

K. Complete
Be sure recipient has knowledge and experience sufficient to carry out order. Give illustrations and examples.

A DEPARTMENTAL PERSONNEL OFFICE IS RESPONSIBLE FOR THE FOLLOWING FUNCTIONS

1. Policy
2. Personnel Programs
3. Recruitment and Placement
4. Position Classification
5. Salary and Wage Administration
6. Employee performance Standards and Evaluation
7. Employee Relations
8. Disciplinary Actions and Separations
9. Health and Safety
10. Staff Training and Development
11. Personnel Records, Procedures, and Reports
12. Employee Services
13. Personnel Research

SUPERVISION

I. LEADERSHIP

All leadership is based essentially on authority. This comes from two sources: It is received from higher management or it is earned by the supervisor through his methods of supervision. Although effective leadership has always depended upon the leader's using his authority in such a way as to appeal successfully to the motives of the people supervised, the conditions for making this appeal are continually changing. The key to today's problem of leadership is flexibility and resourcefulness on the part of the leader in meeting changes in conditions as they occur.

Three basic approaches to leadership are generally recognized:

A. The Authoritarian Approach
   1. The methods and techniques used in this approach emphasize the *I* in leadership and depend primarily on the formal authority of the leader. This authority is sometimes exercised in a hardboiled manner and sometimes in a benevolent

manner, but in either case the dominating role of the leader is reflected in the thinking, planning, and decisions of the group.

2. Group results are to a large degree dependent on close supervision by the leader. Usually, the individuals in the group will not show a high degree of initiative or acceptance of responsibility and their capacity to grow and develop probably will not be fully utilized. The group may react with resentment or submission, depending upon the manner and skill of the leader in using his authority.
3. This approach develops as a natural outgrowth of the authority that goes with the leader's job and his feeling of sole responsibility for getting the job done. It is relatively easy to use and does not require must resourcefulness.
4. The use of this approach is effective in times of emergencies, in meeting close deadline as a final resort, in settling some issues, in disciplinary matters, and with dependent individuals and groups.

B. The Laissez-Faire or Let 'em Alone Approach

1. This approach generally is characterized by an avoidance of leadership responsibility by the leader. The activities of the group depend largely on the choice of its members rather than the leader.
2. Group results probably will be poor. Generally, there will be disagreements over petty things, bickering, and confusion. Except for a few aggressive people, individuals will not show much initiative and growth and development will be retarded. There may be a tendency for informal leaders to take over leadership of the group.
3. This approach frequently results from the leader's dislike of responsibility, from his lack of confidence, from failure of other methods to work, from disappointment or criticism. It is usually the easiest of the three to use and requires both understanding and resourcefulness on the part of the leader.
4. This approach is occasionally useful and effective, particularly in forcing dependent individuals or groups to rely on themselves, to give someone a chance to save face by clearing his own difficulties, or when action should be delayed temporarily for good cause.

C. The Democratic Approach

1. The methods and techniques used in this approach emphasize the *we* in leadership and build up the responsibility of the group to attain its objectives. Reliance is placed largely on the earned authority of the leader.
2. Group results are likely to be good because most of the job motives of the people will be satisfied. Cooperation and teamwork, initiative, acceptance of responsibility, and the individual's capacity for growth probably will show a high degree of development.
3. This approach grows out of a desire or necessity of the leader to find ways to appeal effectively to the motivation of his group. It is the best approach to build up inside the person a strong desire to cooperate and apply himself to the job. It is the most difficult to develop, and requires both understanding and resourcefulness on the part of the leader.
4. The value of this approach increases over a long period where sustained efficiency and development of people are important. It may not be fully effective in all situations, however, particularly when there is not sufficient time to use it properly or where quick decisions must be made.

All three approaches are used by most leaders and have a place in supervising people. The extent of their use varies with individual leaders, with some using one approach predominantly. The leader who uses these three approaches, and varies their use with time and circumstance, is probably the most effective. Leadership which is used predominantly with a democratic approach requires more resourcefulness on the part of the leader but offers the greatest possibilities in terms of teamwork and cooperation.

The one best way of developing democratic leadership is to provide a real sense of participation on the part of the group, since this satisfies most of the chief job motives. Although there are many ways of providing participation, consulting as frequently as possible with individuals and groups on things that affect them seems to offer the most in building cooperation and responsibility. Consultation takes different forms, but it is most constructive when people feel they are actually helping in finding the answers to the problems on the job.

There are some requirements of leaders in respect to human relations which should be considered in their selection and development. Generally, the leader should be interested in working with other people, emotionally stable, self-confident, and sensitive to the reactions of others. In addition, his viewpoint should be one of getting the job done through people who work cooperatively in response to his leadership. He should have a knowledge of individual and group behavior, but, most important of all, he should work to combine all of these requirements into a definite, practical skill in leadership.

II. NINE POINTS OF CONTRAST BETWEEN *BOSS* AND *LEADER*

A. The boss drives his men; the leader coaches them.
B. The boss depends on authority; the leader on good will.
C. The boss inspires fear; the leader inspires enthusiasm.
D. The boss says I; the leader says *We*.
E. The boss says *Get here on time*; the leader gets there ahead of time.
F. The boss fixes the blame for the breakdown; the leader fixes the breakdown.
G. The boss knows how it is done; the leader shows how.
H. The boss makes work a drudgery; the leader makes work a game.
I. The boss says *Go*; the leader says *Let's go*.

EMPLOYEE MORALE

Employee morale is the way employees feel about each other, the organization or unit in which they work, and the work they perform.

I. SOME WAYS TO DEVELOP AND MAINTAIN GOOD EMPLYEE MORALE

A. Give adequate credit and praise when due.
B. Recognize importance of all jobs and equalize load with proper assignments, always giving consideration to personality differences and abilities.
C. Welcome suggestions and do not have an *all-wise* attitude. Request employees' assistance in solving problems and use assistants when conducting group meetings on certain subjects.
D. Properly assign responsibilities and give adequate authority for fulfillment of such assignments.

E. Keep employees informed about matters that affect them.
F. Criticize and reprimand employees privately.
G. Be accessible and willing to listen.
H. Be fair.
I. Be alert to detect training possibilities so that you will not miss an opportunity to help each employee do a better job, and if possible with less effort on his part.
J. Set a good example.
K. Apply the golden rule.

II. SOME INDICATIONS OF GOOD MORALE

A. Good quality of work
B. Good quantity
C. Good attitude of employees
D. Good discipline
E. Teamwork
F. Good attendance
G. Employee participation

MOTIVATION

DRIVES

A drive, stated simply, is a desire or force which causes a person to do or say certain things. These are some of the most usual drives and some of their identifying characteristics recognizable in people motivated by such drives:

A. Security (desire to provide for the future)
Always on time for work
Works for the same employer for many years
Never takes unnecessary chances
Seldom resists doing what he is told

B. Recognition (desire to be rewarded for accomplishment)
Likes to be asked for his opinion
Becomes very disturbed when he makes a mistake
Does things to attract attention
Likes to see his name in print

C. Position (desire to hold certain status in relation to others)
Boasts about important people he knows
Wants to be known as a key man
Likes titles
Demands respect
Belongs to clubs, for prestige

D. Accomplishment (desire to get things done)
Complains when things are held up
Likes to do things that have tangible results
Never lies down on the job
Is proud of turning out good work

E. Companionship (desire to associate with other people)
Likes to work with others
Tells stories and jokes
Indulges in horseplay
Finds excuses to talk to others on the job

F. Possession (desire to collect and hoard objects)
Likes to collect things
Puts his name on things belonging to him
Insists on the same location

Supervisors may find that identifying the drives of employees is a helpful step toward motivating them to self-improvement and better job performance. For example: An employee's job performance is below average. His supervisor, having previously determined that the employee is motivated by a drive for security, suggests that taking training courses will help the employee to improve, advance, and earn more money. Since earning more money can be a step toward greater security, the employee's drive for security would motivate him to take the training suggested by the supervisor. In essence, this is the process of charting an employee's future course by using his motivating drives to positive advantage.

EMPLOYEE PARTICIPATION

I. WHAT IS PARTICIPATION

Employee participation is the employee's giving freely of his time, skill, and knowledge to an extent which cannot be obtained by demand.

II. WHY IS IT IMPORTANT?

The supervisor's responsibility is to get the job done through people. A good supervisor gets the job done through people who work willingly and well. The participation of employees is important because:

A. Employees develop a greater sense of responsibility when they share in working out operating plans and goals.
B. Participation provides greater opportunity and stimulation for employees to learn, and to develop their ability.
C. Participation sometimes provides better solutions to problems because such solutions may combine the experience and knowledge of interested employees who want the solutions to work.
D. An employee or group may offer a solution which the supervisor might hesitate to make for fear of demanding too much.

E. Since the group wants to make the solution work, they exert pressure in a constructive way on each other.
F. Participation usually results in reducing the need for close supervision.

II. HOW MAY SUPERVISORS OBTAIN IT?

Participation is encouraged when employees feel that they share some responsibility for the work and that their ideas are sincerely wanted and valued. Some ways of obtaining employee participation are:

A. Conduct orientation programs for new employees to inform them about the organization and their rights and responsibilities as employees.
B. Explain the aims and objectives of the agency. On a continuing basis, be sure that the employees know what these aims and objectives are.
C. Share job successes and responsibilities and give credit for success.
D. Consult with employees, both as individuals and in groups, about things that affect them.
E. Encourage suggestions for job improvements. Help employees to develop good suggestions. The suggestions can bring them recognition. The city's suggestion program offers additional encouragement through cash awards.

The supervisor who encourages employee participation is not surrendering his authority. He must still make decisions and initiate action, and he must continue to be ultimately responsible for the work of those he supervises. But, through employee participation, he is helping his group to develop greater ability and a sense of responsibility while getting the job done faster and better.

STEPS IN HANDLING A GRIEVANCE

1. Get the Facts
   a. Listen sympathetically
   b. Let him talk himself out
   c. Get his story straight
   d. Get his point of view
   e. Don't argue with him
   f. Give him plenty of time
   g. Conduct the interview privately
   h. Don't try to shift the blame or pass the buck

2. Consider the Facts
   a. Consider the employee's viewpoint
   b. How will the decision affect similar cases
   c. Consider each decision as a possible precedent
   d. Avoid snap judgments—don't jump to conclusions

3. Make or Get a Decision
   a. Frame an effective counter-proposal
   b. Make sure it is fair to all
   c. Have confidence in your judgment
   d. Be sure you can substantiate your decision

4. Notify the Employee of Your Decision
   Be sure he is told; try to convince him that the decision is fair and just.

5. Take Action When Needed and If Within Your Authority
   Otherwise, tell employee that the matter will be called to the attention of the proper person or that nothing can be done, and why it cannot.

6. Follow through to see that the desired result is achieved.

7. Record key facts concerning the complaint and the action taken.

8. Leave the way open to him to appeal your decision to a higher authority.

9. Report all grievances to your superior, whether they are appealed or not.

DISCIPLINE

Discipline is training that develops self-control, orderly conduct, and efficiency.

To discipline does not necessarily mean to punish.

To discipline does mean to train, to regulate, and to govern conduct.

I. THE DISCIPLINARY INTERVIEW

Most employees sincerely want to do what is expected of them. In other words, they are self-disciplined. Some employees, however, fail to observe established rules and standards, and disciplinary action by the supervisor is required.

The primary purpose of disciplinary action is to improve conduct without creating dissatisfaction, bitterness, or resentment in the process.

Constructive disciplinary action is more concerned with causes and explanations of breaches of conduct than with punishment. The disciplinary interview is held to get at the causes of apparent misbehavior and to motivate better performance in the future.

It is important that the interview be kept on an impersonal a basis as possible. If the supervisor lets the interview descend to the plane of an argument, it loses its effectiveness.

II. PLANNING THE INTERVIEW

Get all pertinent facts concerning the situation so that you can talk in specific terms to the employee.

Review the employee's record, appraisal ratings, etc.

Consider what you know about the temperament of the employee. Consider your attitude toward the employee. Remember that the primary requisite of disciplinary action is fairness.

Don't enter upon the interview when angry.

Schedule the interview for a place which is private and out of hearing of others.

III. CONDUCTING THE INTERVIEW

A. Make an effort to establish accord.
B. Question the employee about the apparent breach of discipline. Be sure that the question is not so worded as to be itself an accusation.
C. Give the employee a chance to tell his side of the story. Give him ample opportunity to talk.
D. Use understanding—listening except where it is necessary to ask a question or to point out some details of which the employee may not be aware. If the employee misrepresents facts, make a plain, accurate statement of the facts, but don't argue and don't engage in personal controversy.
E. Listen and try to understand the reasons for the employee's (mis)conduct. First of all, don't assume that there has been a breach of discipline. Evaluate the employee's reasons for his conduct in the light of his opinions and feelings concerning the consistency and reasonableness of the standards which he was expected to follow. Has the supervisor done his part in explaining the reasons for the rule? Was the employee's behavior unintentional or deliberate? Does he think he had real reasons for his actions? What new facts is he telling? Do the facts justify his actions? What causes, other than those mentioned, could have stimulated the behavior?
F. After listening to the employee's version of the situation, and if censure of his actions is warranted, the supervisor should proceed with whatever criticism is justified. Emphasis should be placed on future improvement rather than exclusively on the employee's failure to measure up to expected standards of job conduct.
G. Fit the criticism to the individual. With one employee, a word of correction may be all that is required.
H. Attempt to distinguish between unintentional error and deliberate misbehavior. An error due to ignorance requires training and not censure.
I. Administer criticism in a controlled, even tone of voice, never in anger. Make it clear that you are acting as an agent of the department. In general, criticism should refer to the job or the employee's actions and not to the person. Criticism of the employee's work is not an attack on the individual.
J. Be sure the interview does not destroy the employee's self-confidence. Mention his good qualities and assure him that you feel confident that he can improve his performance.
K. Wherever possible, before the employee leaves the interview, satisfy him that the incident is closed, that nothing more will be said on the subject unless the offense is repeated.

www.ingramcontent.com/pod-product-compliance
Lightning Source LLC
Chambersburg PA
CBHW081816300426
44116CB00014B/2382
* 9 7 8 1 7 9 9 3 1 0 7 7 8 *